D0074692

Stand Out
Basic

Standards-Based English

Rob Jenkins
Staci Johnson

Australia • Brazil • Japan • Korea • Mexico • Singapore • Spain • United Kingdom • United States

HEINLE
CENGAGE Learning™

Stand Out Basic
Standards-Based English
Rob Jenkins and Staci Johnson

Editorial Director: Joe Dougherty

Publisher, ESL and Dictionaries: Sherrise Roehr

Acquisitions Editor: Tom Jefferies

VP, Director of Content Development:
  Anita Raducanu

Developmental Editor: John Hicks

Associate Media Development Editor:
  Jonelle Lonergan

Director of Product Marketing: Amy T. Mabley

Executive Marketing Manager, U.S.:
  Jim McDonough

Senior Field Marketing Manager:
  Donna Lee Kennedy

Product Marketing Manager: Katie Kelley

Content Project Manager: Dawn Marie Elwell

Senior Print Buyer: Mary Beth Hennebury

Developmental Editor: Kasia McNabb

Project Manager: Tunde Dewey

Composition: Pre-Press PMG

Cover and Interior Design: Studio Montage

Illustrators: James Edwards, S.I. International

Cover Art: ©Lisa Henderling/Getty Images

© 2008 Heinle, Cengage Learning

ALL RIGHTS RESERVED. No part of this work covered by the copyright herein may be reproduced, transmitted, stored or used in any form or by any means graphic, electronic, or mechanical, including but not limited to photocopying, recording, scanning, digitizing, taping, Web distribution, information networks, or information storage and retrieval systems, except as permitted under Section 107 or 108 of the 1976 United States Copyright Act, without the prior written permission of the publisher.

For permission to use material from this text or product, submit all requests online at **www.cengage.com/permissions**
Further permissions questions can be emailed to **permissionrequest@cengage.com**

Library of Congress Control Number: 2007930964

ISBN-13: 978-1-4240-0254-2

ISBN-10: 1-4240-0254-0

Heinle
20 Channel Center Street
Boston, MA 02210
USA

Cengage Learning is a leading provider of customized learning solutions with office locations around the globe, including Singapore, the United Kingdom, Australia, Mexico, Brazil, and Japan. Locate your local office at **www.cengage.com/global**

Cengage Learning products are represented in Canada by Nelson Education, Ltd.

Visit Heinle online at **elt.heinle.com**
Visit our corporate website at **www.cengage.com**

Printed in the United States of America
5 6 7 15 14 13

ACKNOWLEDGMENTS

Elizabeth Aderman
New York City Board of Education, New York, NY

Sharon Baker
Roseville Adult School, Roseville, CA

Lillian Barredo
Stockton School for Adults, Stockton, CA

Linda Boice
Elk Grove Adult Education, Elk Grove, CA

Chan Bostwick
Los Angeles Unified School District, Los Angeles, CA

Debra Brooks
Manhattan BEGIN Program, New York, NY

Anne Byrnes
North Hollywood-Polytechnic Community Adult School, Sun Valley, CA

Rose Cantu
John Jay High School, San Antonio, TX

Toni Chapralis
Fremont School for Adults, Sacramento, CA

Melanie Chitwood
Miami-Dade College, Miami, FL

Geri Creamer
Stockton School for Adults, Stockton, CA

Stephanie Daubar
Harry W. Brewster Technical Center, Tampa, FL

Irene Dennis
San Antonio College, San Antonio, TX

Eileen Duffell
P.S. 64, New York, NY

Nancy Dunlap
Northside Independent School District, San Antonio, TX

Gloria Eriksson
Old Marshall Adult Education Center, Sacramento, CA

Marti Estrin
Santa Rosa Junior College, Santa Rosa, CA

Lawrence Fish
Shorefront YM-YWHA English Language Program, Brooklyn, NY

Victoria Florit
Miami-Dade College, Miami, FL

Rhoda Gilbert
New York City Board of Education, New York, NY

Kathleen Jimenez
Miami-Dade College, Miami, FL

Nancy Jordan
John Jay High School Adult Education, San Antonio, TX

Renee Klosz
Lindsey Hopkins Technical Education Center, Miami, FL

David Lauter
Stockton School for Adults, Stockton, CA

Patricia Long
Old Marshall Adult Education Center, Sacramento, CA

Daniel Loos
Seattle Community College, Seattle, WA

Maria Miranda
Lindsey Hopkins Technical Education Center, Miami, FL

Karen Moore
Stockton School for Adults, Stockton, CA

George Myskiw
Malcolm X College, Chicago, IL

Heidi Perez
Lawrence Public Schools Adult Learning Center, Lawrence, MA

Marta Pitt
Lindsey Hopkins Technical Education Center, Miami, FL

Sylvia Rambach
Stockton School for Adults, Stockton, CA

Eric Rosenbaum
BEGIN Managed Programs, New York, NY

Laura Rowley
Old Marshall Adult Education Center, Sacramento, CA

Stephanie Schmitter
Mercer County Community College, Trenton, NJ

Amy Schneider
Pacoima Skills Center, Pacoima, CA

Sr. M. B. Theresa Spittle
Stockton School for Adults, Stockton, CA

Andre Sutton
Belmont Adult School, Los Angeles, CA

Jennifer Swoyer
Northside Independent School District, San Antonio, TX

Claire Valier
Palm Beach County School District, West Palm Beach, FL

Rob Jenkins

Staci Johnson

I love teaching. I love to see the expressions on my students' faces when the light goes on and their eyes show such sincere joy of learning. I knew the first time I stepped into an ESL classroom that this was where I needed to be and I have never questioned that resolution. I have worked in business, sales, and publishing, and I've found challenge in all, but nothing can compare to the satisfaction of reaching people in such a personal way.

Ever since I can remember, I've been fascinated with other cultures and languages. I love to travel and every place I go, the first thing I want to do is meet the people, learn their language, and understand their culture. Becoming an ESL teacher was a perfect way to turn what I love to do into my profession. There's nothing more incredible than the exchange of teaching and learning from one another that goes on in an ESL classroom. And there's nothing more rewarding than helping a student succeed.

We are so happy that instructors and agencies have embraced the lesson planning and project-based activities that we introduced in the first edition and are so enthusiastically teaching with **Stand Out**. It is fantastic that so many of our colleagues are as excited to be in this profession as we are. After writing over 500 lesson plans and implementing them in our own classrooms and after personal discussions with thousands of instructors all over the United States and in different parts of the world, we have found ourselves in a position to improve upon our successful model. One of the most notable things in the new edition is that we have continued to stress integrating skills in each lesson and have made this integration more apparent and obvious. To accomplish any life skill, students need to incorporate a combination of reading, writing, listening, speaking, grammar, pronunciation, and academic skills while developing vocabulary and these skills should be taught together in a lesson! We have accomplished this by extending the presentation of lessons in the book, so each lesson is more fully developed. You will also notice an extended list of ancillaries and a tighter correlation of these ancillaries to each book. The ancillaries allow you to extend practice on particular skill areas beyond the lesson in the text. We are so excited about this curriculum and know that as you implement it, you and your students will *stand out*.

Our goal is to give students challenging opportunities to be successful in their language-learning experience so they develop confidence and become independent, lifelong learners.

Rob Jenkins
Staci Johnson

ABOUT THE SERIES

The **Stand Out** series is designed to facilitate *active* learning while challenging students to build a nurturing and effective learning community.

The student books are divided into eight distinct units, mirroring competency areas most useful to newcomers. These areas are outlined in CASAS assessment programs and different state model standards for adults. Each unit in *Stand Out Basic* is then divided into five lessons, a review, and a team project. Lessons are driven by performance objectives and are filled with challenging activities that progress from teacher-presented to student-centered tasks.

SUPPLEMENTAL MATERIALS

- The *Stand Out Basic Lesson Planner* is in full color with 60 complete lesson plans, taking the instructor through each stage of a lesson from warm-up and review through application.

- The *Stand Out Basic Activity Bank CD-ROM* has an abundance of customizable worksheets. Print or download and modify what you need for your particular class.

- The *Stand Out Basic Grammar Challenge* is a workbook that gives additional grammar explanation and practice in context.

- The *Stand Out ExamView® Test Bank CD-ROM* allows you to customize pre- and post-tests for each unit as well as a pre- and post-test for the book.

- Listening scripts are found in the back of the student book and the Lesson Planner. CDs are available with focused listening activities described in the Lesson Planner.

STAND OUT BASIC LESSON PLANNER

The *Stand Out Basic Lesson Planner* is a new and innovative approach. As many seasoned teachers know, good lesson planning can make a substantial difference in the classroom. Students continue coming to class, understanding, applying, and remembering more of what they learn. They are more confident in their learning when good lesson planning techniques are incorporated.

We have developed lesson plans that are designed to be used each day and to reduce preparation time. The planner includes:

- Standard lesson progression (Warm-up and Review, Introduction, Presentation, Practice, Evaluation, and Application)

- A creative and complete way to approach varied class lengths so that each lesson will work within a class period.

- 180 hours of classroom activities
- Time suggestions for each activity
- Pedagogical comments
- Space for teacher notes and future planning
- Identification of SCANS and CASAS standards

USER QUESTIONS ABOUT STAND OUT

- **What are SCANS and how do they integrate into the book?**
  SCANS is the Secretary's Commission on Achieving Necessary Skills. SCANS was developed to encourage students to prepare for the workplace. The standards developed through SCANS have been incorporated throughout the **Stand Out** student books and components.

  Stand Out addresses SCANS a little differently than do other books. SCANS standards elicit effective teaching strategies by incorporating essential skills such as critical thinking and group work. We have incorporated SCANS standards in every lesson, not isolating these standards in the work unit, as is typically done.

- **What about CASAS?** The federal government has mandated that states show student outcomes as a prerequisite to receiving funding. Some states have incorporated the **C**omprehensive **A**dult **S**tudent **A**ssessment **S**ystem (CASAS) testing to standardize agency reporting. Unfortunately, since many of our students are unfamiliar with standardized testing and therefore struggle with it, adult schools need to develop lesson plans to address specific concerns. **Stand Out** was developed with careful attention to CASAS skill areas in most lessons and performance objectives.

- **Are the tasks too challenging for my students?**
  Students learn by doing and learn more when challenged. **Stand Out** provides tasks that encourage critical thinking in a variety of ways. The tasks in each lesson move from teacher-directed to student-centered so the learner clearly understands what's expected and is willing to "take a risk." The lessons are expected to be challenging. In this way, students learn that when they work together as a learning community, anything becomes possible. The satisfaction of accomplishing something both as an individual and as a member of a team results in greater confidence and effective learning.

- **Do I need to understand lesson planning to teach from the student book?** If you don't understand lesson planning when you start, you will when you finish! Teaching from **Stand Out** is like a course on lesson planning, especially if you use the Lesson Planner on a daily basis.

Stand Out does *stand out* because, when we developed this series, we first established performance objectives for each lesson. Then we designed lesson plans, followed by student book pages. The introduction to each lesson varies because different objectives demand different approaches. **Stand Out's** variety of tasks makes learning more interesting for the student.

- **What are team projects?** The final lesson of each unit is a **team project**. This is often a team simulation that incorporates the objectives of the unit and provides an additional opportunity for students to actively apply what they have learned. The project allows students to produce something that represents their progress in learning. These end-of-unit projects were created with a variety of learning styles and individual skills in mind. The team projects can be skipped or simplified, but we encourage instructors to implement them, enriching the overall student experience.

- **What do you mean by a customizable Activity Bank?** Every class, student, teacher, and approach is different. Since no one textbook can meet all these differences, the *Stand Out Activity Bank CD-ROM* allows you to customize **Stand Out** for your class. You can copy different activities and worksheets from the CD-ROM to your hard drive and then:

  - change items in supplemental vocabulary, grammar, and life skill activities;
  - personalize activities with student names and popular locations in your area;
  - extend every lesson with additional practice where you feel it is most needed.

- **Is *Stand Out* grammar-based or competency-based?** **Stand Out** is a competency-based series; however, students are exposed to basic grammar structures. We believe that

grammar instruction in context is extremely important. Grammar structures are periodically identified as principal lesson objectives. Students are first provided with context that incorporates the grammar, followed by an explanation and practice. At this level, we expect students to learn basic structures but we do not expect them to acquire them. It has been our experience that students are exposed several times within their learning experience to language structures before they actually acquire them. For teachers who want to enhance grammar instruction, the *Activity Bank CD-ROM* and/or the *Grammar Challenge* workbooks provide ample opportunities.

The six competencies that drive **Stand Out** are basic communication, consumer economics, community resources, health, occupational knowledge, and lifelong learning (government and law replace lifelong learning in Books 3 and 4).

- **Are there enough activities so I don't have to supplement?** **Stand Out** stands alone in providing 180 hours of instruction and activities, even without the additional suggestions in the Lesson Planner. The Lesson Planner also shows you how to streamline lessons to provide 90 hours of classwork and still have thorough lessons if you meet less often. When supplementing with the *Stand Out Activity Bank CD-ROM*, the Exam*View*® *Test Bank CD-ROM*, and the *Stand Out Grammar Challenge* workbook, you gain unlimited opportunities to extend class hours and provide activities related directly to each lesson objective. Calculate how many hours your class meets in a semester and look to **Stand Out** to address the full class experience.

Stand Out is a comprehensive approach to adult language learning, meeting needs of students and instructors completely and effectively.

CONTENTS

	Numeracy/ Academic Skills	EFF	SCANS	CASAS
Pre-Unit	· Writing numerals 1-9 · Writing telephone numbers · Dictation · Focused listening · Class application · Test-taking skills	· Speak so others can understand · Listen actively	**Many SCAN skills are incorporated in this unit with an emphasis on:** · Listening · Speaking · Writing · Sociability · Acquiring and evaluating information · Interpreting and communicating information	**1:** 0.1.1, 0.1.4, 0.2.1 **2:** 0.1.1, 0.1.4, 0.2.1 **3:** 0.1.5, 7.4.7 **R:** 7.4.1, 7.4.2, 7.4.3
Unit 1	· Writing numerals 1-31 · Writing dates · Focused listening · Teamwork skills · Reviewing · Evaluating · Developing study skills	· Speak so others can understand · Listen actively · Cooperate with others	**Many SCAN skills are incorporated in this unit with an emphasis on:** · Basic skills · Acquiring and evaluating information · Interpreting and communicating information · Seeing things in the mind's eye · Sociability	**1:** 0.1.1, 0.2.1 **2:** 0.1.2, 0.2.1, 1.1.3, 4.8.7 **3:** 0.1.2, 0.2.1 **4:** 0.1.2, 0.2.1, 1.1.3, 4.8.7 **5:** 0.1.2, 0.2.1, 2.3.2 **R:** 0.1.1, 0.2.1, 7.4.1, 7.4.2, 7.4.3 **TP:** 0.1.1, 0.2.1, 4.8.1
Unit 2	· Interpreting a bar graph · Telling time · Focused listening · Scheduling · Reviewing · Evaluating · Developing study skills	· Read with understanding · Convey ideas in writing · Speak so others can understand · Listen Actively · Cooperate with others · Observe critically · Take responsibility for learning	**Many SCAN skills are incorporated in this unit with an emphasis on:** · Acquiring and evaluating information · Organizing and maintaining information · Interpreting and communicating information · Basic skills · Reflect and Evaluate	**1:** 0.1.4 **2:** 0.1.5 **3:** 0.1.5 **4:** 0.2.1, 0.2.4, 2.3.1 **5:** 0.1.2, 0.2.1, 1.1.3, 2.3.3 **R:** 0.1.5, 2.3.1, 2.3.2, 2.3.3, 7.4.1, 7.4.2, 7.4.3 **TP:** 0.1.5, 2.3.1, 2.3.2, 2.3.3, 4.8.1

CONTENTS

● Grammar points that are explicitly taught   ◊ Grammar points that are presented in context   △ Grammar points that are being recycled

Numeracy/ Academic Skills	EFF	SCANS	CASAS
Unit 3 · Using U.S. measurements: pounds, gallons · Working in a group · Focused listening · Skimming · Categorizing and organizing information · Teamwork skills · Reviewing · Evaluating · Developing study skills	· Read with understanding · Convey ideas in writing · Speak so others can understand · Listen actively · Cooperate with others · Take responsibility for learning · Reflect and evaluate	**Many SCAN skills are incorporated in this unit with an emphasis on:** ◊ Acquiring and evaluating information ◊ Organizing and maintaining information ◊ Interpreting and communicating information · Allocating human resources · Basic skills · Seeing things in the mind's eye	**1:** 1.3.8 **2:** 1.3.8 **3:** 1.1.1, 1.3.8 **4:** 1.3.8 **5:** 1.3.8 **R:** 1.3.8, 7.4.1, 7.4.2, 7.4.3 **TP:** 1.88, 4.8.1
Unit 4 · Using U.S. measurements: clothing sizes · Maintaining inventories · Counting U.S. money · Calculating totals · Writing checks · Asking for information ' · Focused listening · Test-taking skills · Reviewing · Evaluating · Developing study skills	· Read with understanding · Convey ideas in writing · Speak so others can understand · Listen actively · Cooperate with others · Observe critically · Use math · Take responsibility for learning · Reflect and evaluate · Observe critically · Guide others	**Many SCAN skills are incorporated in this unit with an emphasis on:** · Acquiring and evaluating information · Organizing and maintaining information · Interpreting and communicating information · Basic skills · Allocating money · Serving clients and customers	**1:** 1.3.9 **2:** 1.1.9, 1.2.1, 1.3.9 **3:** 1.1.9, 1.2.1, 1.3.9 **4:** 1.1.6, 1.3.9, 4.8.1, 6.1.1 **5:** 1.1.9, 1.2.1, 1.3.9, 4.8.3 **R:** 1.1.9, 1.2.1, 1.3.9, 7.4.1, 7.4.2, 7.4.3 **TP:** 1.3.9, 4.8.1
Unit 5 · Interpreting a bar graph · Creating a bar graph · Test-taking strategies · Focused listening · Dictation · Reviewing · Evaluating · Developing study skills	· Read with understanding · Convey ideas in writing · Speak so others can understand · Listen actively · Cooperate with others · Observe critically · Take responsibility for learning · Reflect and evaluate · Solve problems and make decisions	**Many SCAN skills are incorporated in this unit with an emphasis on:** · Acquiring and evaluating information · Organizing and maintaining information · Interpreting and communicating information · Basic skills · Creative thinking · Participating as a member of a team	**1:** 1.3.7, 7.2.3 **2:** 1.4.1, 1.4.2, 1.9.4 **3:** 1.1.3, 2.2.3, 2.2.5, 6.7.2 **4:** 0.1.2, 0.2.4 **5:** 1.1.3, 1.9.1, 1.9.4, 2.2.1, 2.2.2, 2.5.4 **R:** 2.2.3, 7.4.1, 7.4.2, 7.4.3 **TP:** 2.2.3, 4.8.1

CONTENTS

· Grammar points that are explicitly taught   ◊ Grammar points that are presented in context   △ Grammar points that are being recycled

Numeracy/Academic Skills	EFF	SCANS	CASAS
Unit 6 · Focused listening · Test-taking skills · Reviewing · Evaluating · Developing study skills	· Read with understanding · Convey ideas in writing · Speak so others can understand · Listen actively · Cooperate with others · Observe critically · Take responsibility for learning · Reflect and evaluate · Advocate and influence	**Many SCAN skills are incorporated in this unit with an emphasis on:** · Acquiring and evaluating information · Organizing and maintaining information · Interpreting and communicating information · Basic skills · Self-management · Responsibility	**1:** 3.1.1, 3.1.3 **2:** 0.1.2, 0.2.1, 3.1.1 **3:** 2.3.1, 3.1.2, 3.3.1 **4:** 3.1.1 **5:** 3.1.3 **R:** 3.1.1, 3.1.2, 3.1.3, 3.3.1 **TP:** 1.3.9, 4.8.1
Unit 7 · Focused listening · Making graphs · Reviewing · Evaluating · Developing study skills	· Read with understanding · Convey ideas in writing · Speak so others can understand · Listen actively · Cooperate with others · Advocate and influence · Resolve conflict and negotiate · Observe critically · Take responsibility for learning · Reflect and evaluate	**Many SCAN skills are incorporated in this unit with an emphasis on:** · Acquiring and evaluating information · Organizing and maintaining information · Interpreting and communicating information · Basic skills · Self-management	**1:** 0.2.1, 4.1.8 **2:** 0.1.6, 4.8.1 **3:** 4.1.3, 4.1.8, 4.4.4 **4:** 4.4.4 **5:** 4.4.4, 4.8.1, 4.8.3 **R:** 4.1.3, 4.1.8, 4.4.1, 4.8.1, 4.8.3, 7.4.1, 7.4.2, 7.4.3 **TP:** 2.2.3, 4.8.1.
Unit 8 · Identifying quantities and sizes · Calculating totals · Reading telephone numbers · Interpreting a bar graph · Focused listening · Test-taking skills · Organizational skills · Reviewing · Evaluating · Developing study skills	· Read with understanding · Convey ideas in writing · Speak so others can understand · Listen actively · Cooperate with others · Resolve conflict and negotiate · Observe critically · Take responsibility for learning · Reflect and evaluate	**Many SCAN skills are incorporated in this unit with an emphasis on:** · Acquiring and evaluating information · Organizing and maintaining information · Interpreting and communicating information · Basic skills · Self-management	**1:** 0.2.1, 0.2.2, 7.1.4 **2:** 1.1.6, 1.2.1, 1.3.1, 1.6.4, 7.1.4 **3:** 2.1.1, 2.2.1, 7.1.4 **4:** 0.2.1, 3.5.9, 6.7.2, 7.1.1, 7.1.2, 7.1.4 **5:** 4.1.1, 4.4.4, 7.1.1, 7.1.4 **R:** 7.4.2, 7.4.3 **TP:** 2.2.3, 4.8.1

Welcome to Stand Out, Second Edition

Stand Out works.

And now it works even better!

Built from the standards necessary for adult English learners, the second edition of *Stand Out* gives students the foundation and tools they need to develop confidence and become independent, lifelong learners.

- **Grammar** Charts clearly explain grammar points, and are followed by personalized exercises.
- **Pronunciation** activities are integrated through the program.

- Clearly defined **goals** provide a roadmap of learning for the student.
- State and federally required **life skills and competencies** are taught, helping students meet necessary benchmarks.

- A variety of **examples from real life**, like bank checks, newspaper ads, money, etc. help students learn to access information and resources in their community.

- Key **vocabulary** is introduced visually and orally.

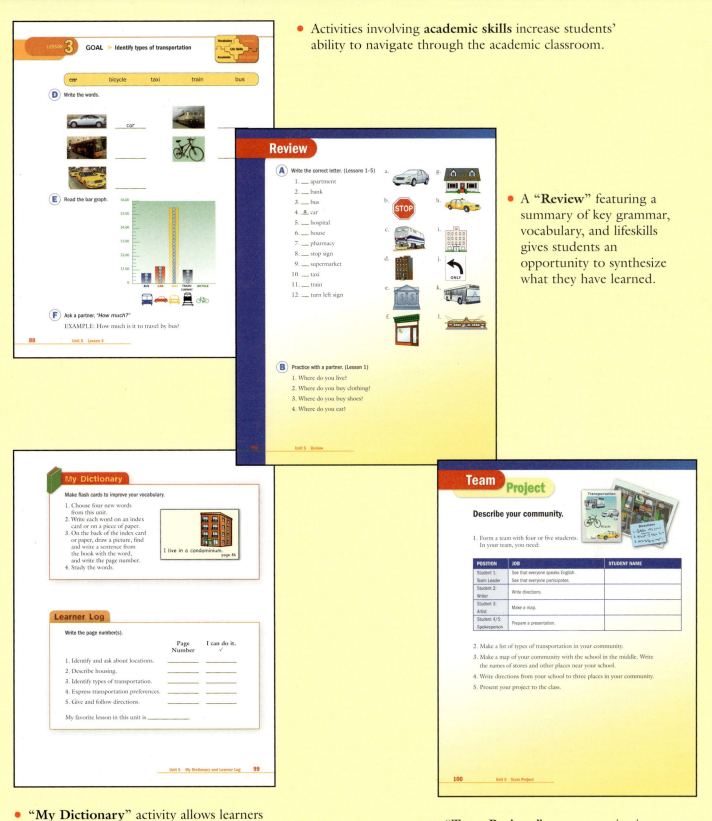

- Activities involving **academic skills** increase students' ability to navigate through the academic classroom.

- A **"Review"** featuring a summary of key grammar, vocabulary, and lifeskills gives students an opportunity to synthesize what they have learned.

- **"My Dictionary"** activity allows learners to use the vocabulary from the unit in a new way, increasing the likelihood that they will acquire the words.
- **"Learner Log"** provides opportunities for learner self-assessment.

- **"Team Projects"** present motivating cross-ability activities which group learners of different levels together to complete a task that applies the unit objective.

The ground-breaking *Stand Out* **Lesson Planners** take the guesswork out of meeting the standards while offering high-interest, meaningful language activities, and three levels of pacing for each book.

- An at-a-glance **agenda** and **prep section** for each lesson ensure that instructors have a clear knowledge of what will be covered in the lesson.

- A complete **lesson plan** for each page in the student book is provided, following a standard lesson progression (Warm-up and Review, Introduction, Presentation, Practice, Evaluation, and Application).

- Clear, easy-to-identify **pacing guide** icons offer three different pacing strategies.

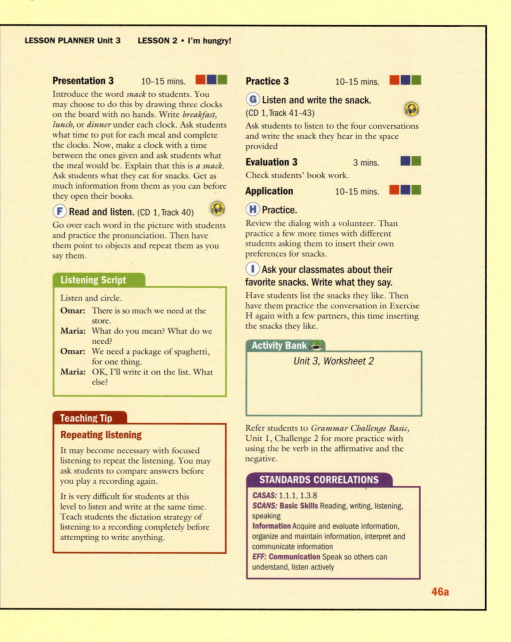

LESSON PLANNER Unit 3   LESSON 2 • I'm hungry!

Presentation 3   10–15 mins.

Introduce the word *snack* to students. You may choose to do this by drawing three clocks on the board with no hands. Write *breakfast, lunch,* or *dinner* under each clock. Ask students what time to put for each meal and complete the clocks. Now, make a clock with a time between the ones given and ask students what the meal would be. Explain that this is *a snack.* Ask students what they eat for snacks. Get as much information from them as you can before they open their books.

F **Read and listen.** (CD 1, Track 40)

Go over each word in the picture with students and practice the pronunciation. Then have them point to objects and repeat them as you say them.

Listening Script

Listen and circle.

Omar: There is so much we need at the store.

Maria: What do you mean? What do we need?

Omar: We need a package of spaghetti, for one thing.

Maria: OK, I'll write it on the list. What else?

Teaching Tip

Repeating listening

It may become necessary with focused listening to repeat the listening. You may ask students to compare answers before you play a recording again.

It is very difficult for students at this level to listen and write at the same time. Teach students the dictation strategy of listening to a recording completely before attempting to write anything.

Practice 3   10–15 mins.

G **Listen and write the snack.**

(CD 1, Track 41–43)

Ask students to listen to the four conversations and write the snack they hear in the space provided

Evaluation 3   3 mins.

Check students' book work.

Application   10–15 mins.

H **Practice.**

Review the dialog with a volunteer. Than practice a few more times with different students asking them to insert their own preferences for snacks.

I Ask your classmates about their favorite snacks. Write what they say.

Have students list the snacks they like. Then have them practice the conversation in Exercise H again with a few partners, this time inserting the snacks they like.

Activity Bank

Unit 3, Worksheet 2

Refer students to *Grammar Challenge Basic,* Unit 1, Challenge 2 for more practice with using the be verb in the affirmative and the negative.

STANDARDS CORRELATIONS

CASAS: 1.1.1, 1.3.8
SCANS: Basic Skills Reading, writing, listening, speaking
Information Acquire and evaluate information, organize and maintain information, interpret and communicate information
EFF: Communication Speak so others can understand, listen actively

46a

- "Teaching Tips" provide ideas and strategies for the classroom.
- Additional **supplemental activities** found on the *Activity Bank CD-ROM* are suggested at their point of use.
- The *Activity Bank CD-ROM* includes **reproducible multilevel activity masters** for each lesson that can be printed or downloaded and modified for classroom needs.
- "Listening Scripts" from the *Audio CD* are included.
- "Standards Correlations" appear directly on the page, detailing how *Stand Out* meets CASAS, EFF, and SCANS standards.

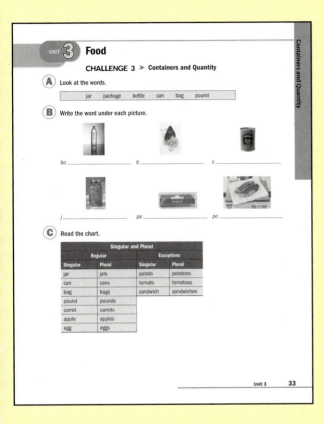

- • *** *Grammar Challenge*** workbooks include supplemental activities for students who desire even more contextual grammar and vocabulary practice.
- • Clear and concise **grammar explanation boxes** provide a strong foundation for the activities.

- • A variety of **activities** allow students develop their grammar skills and apply them.
- • Written by **Rob Jenkins and Staci Johnson**, the *Grammar Challenge* workbooks are directly aligned to the student books.

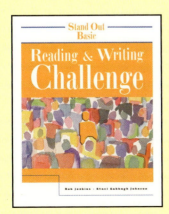

- • *Reading & Writing Challenge* workbooks are also available. These workbooks provide challenging materials and exercises for students who want even more practice in reading, vocabulary development, and writing.

Welcome to Our Class

GOALS

➤ Greet your classmates
➤ Say and write phone numbers
➤ Follow classroom instructions

LESSON **1**

Say hello!

GOAL ➤ Greet your classmates

Vocabulary   Grammar
Life Skills
Academic   Pronunciation

A Listen.

CD 1
TR 1-2

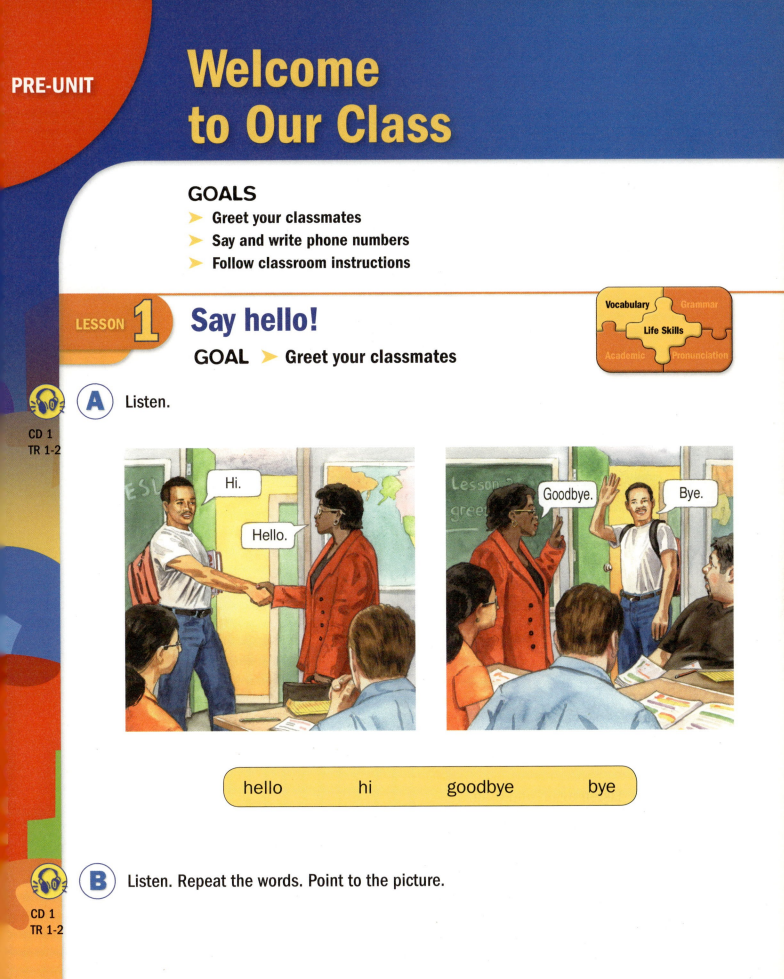

hello   hi   goodbye   bye

B Listen. Repeat the words. Point to the picture.

CD 1
TR 1-2

GOAL ➤ **Greet your classmates**

 C Listen and point to the picture. Who is speaking?

CD 1
TR 3-4

Orlando

Mrs. Adams

Amal

Chinh

Pronunciation

CD 1
TR 5

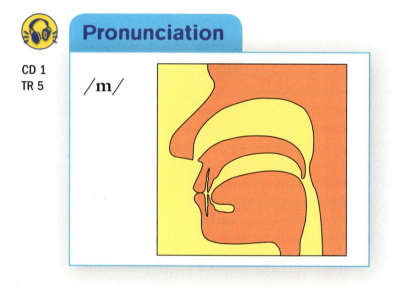

/m/

 D Listen again and read.

CD 1
TR 3-4

Mrs. Adams: Hello. I'm Mrs. Adams.
Orlando: Hi, Mrs. Adams. I'm
Orlando. Nice to meet you.
Mrs. Adams: Nice to meet you, too.
Orlando: Bye.
Mrs. Adams: Goodbye.

Chinh: Hi. I'm Chinh.
Amal: Hello, Chinh. I'm Amal.
Chinh: Nice to meet you.
Amal: Nice to meet you, too.
Chinh: Bye now.
Amal: Bye.

LESSON 1

GOAL ➤ Greet your classmates

Vocabulary | Grammar | Life Skills | Academic | Pronunciation

E Listen and repeat. Then, write.

CD 1
TR 6

Aa Bb Cc Dd Ee Ff Gg Hh Ii

Jj Kk Ll Mm Nn Oo Pp Qq Rr

Ss Tt Uu Vv Ww Xx Yy Zz

I'm Amal.

Contractions

I am = *I'm*

F Write.

hi

hello

goodbye

G Write your name and a classmate's name. Then, meet four more classmates.

Hi. I'm ______________________. (your name)

Hello. I'm ______________________. (classmate's name)

Phone numbers

GOAL ➤ Say and write phone numbers

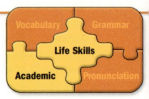

 A Listen and point. Who is speaking?

CD 1
TR 7

 B Listen and repeat. Point to each number. Then, write all the numbers.

CD 1
TR 8

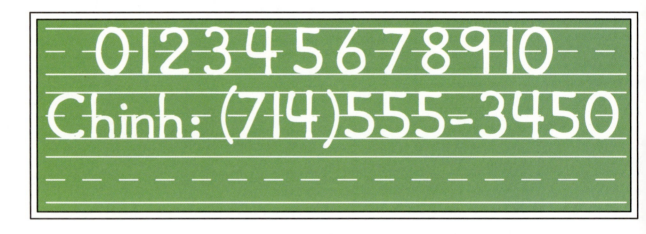

0 1 2 3 4 5 6 7 8 9 10

Chinh: (714) 555-3450

GOAL ➤ **Say and write phone numbers**

Vocabulary · Grammar · Life Skills · Academic · Pronunciation

C Listen to your teacher and write the numbers you hear.

1. _____   5. _____

2. _____   6. _____

3. _____   7. _____

4. _____

D Write your phone number. (___) _____

CD 1
TR 9

E Listen and circle.

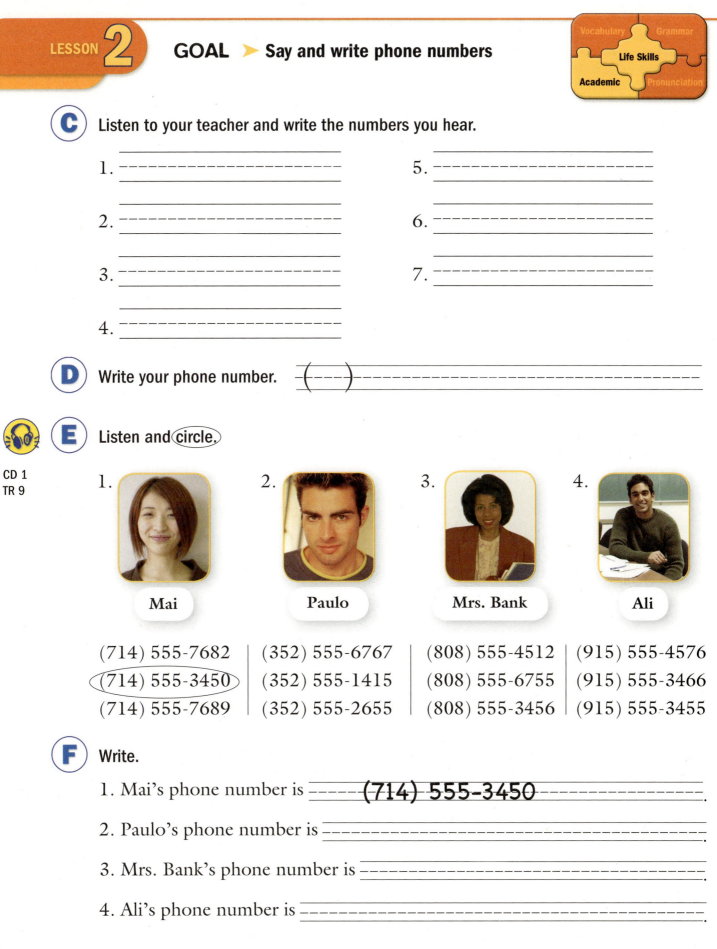

1. **Mai**

(714) 555-7682
(714) 555-3450
(714) 555-7689

2. **Paulo**

(352) 555-6767
(352) 555-1415
(352) 555-2655

3. **Mrs. Bank**

(808) 555-4512
(808) 555-6755
(808) 555-3456

4. **Ali**

(915) 555-4576
(915) 555-3466
(915) 555-3455

F Write.

1. Mai's phone number is __(714) 555-3450__.

2. Paulo's phone number is _____.

3. Mrs. Bank's phone number is _____.

4. Ali's phone number is _____.

GOAL ➤ Say and write phone numbers

G Read the phone list.

PHONE LIST Mrs. Adam's English Class	
Name	**Phone Number**
Chinh	(714) 555-3450
Andre	(714) 555-1333
Shiro	(714) 555-9812
Concepción	(714) 555-4545
Taylor	(714) 555-1237

Be **verb**
I *am* …
The phone number *is* …

H Write the phone numbers.

1. Andre's phone number is _____.

2. Shiro's phone number is _____.

3. Concepción's phone number is _____.

4. Taylor's phone number is _____.

I Make a class phone list.

PHONE LIST	
Name	**Phone Number**
(my name)	

Class work

GOAL ➤ **Follow classroom instructions**

A Listen.

CD 1
TR 10

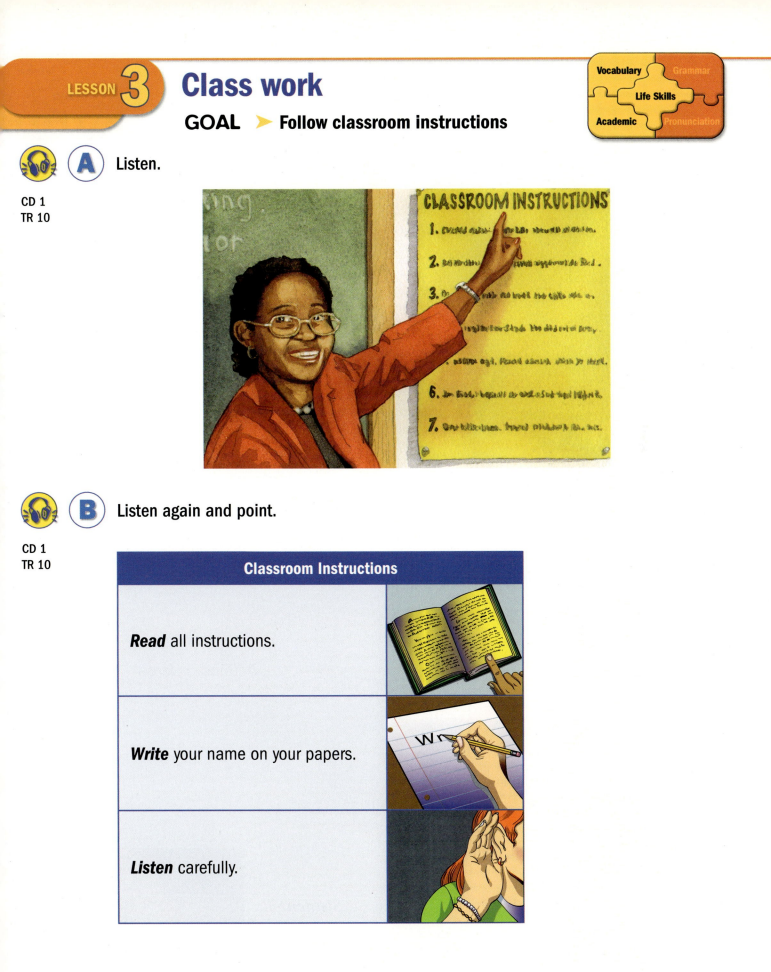

B Listen again and point.

CD 1
TR 10

Classroom Instructions	
Read all instructions.	
Write your name on your papers.	
Listen carefully.	

GOAL ➤ Follow classroom instructions

Vocabulary · Grammar · Life Skills · Academic · Pronunciation

C Write.

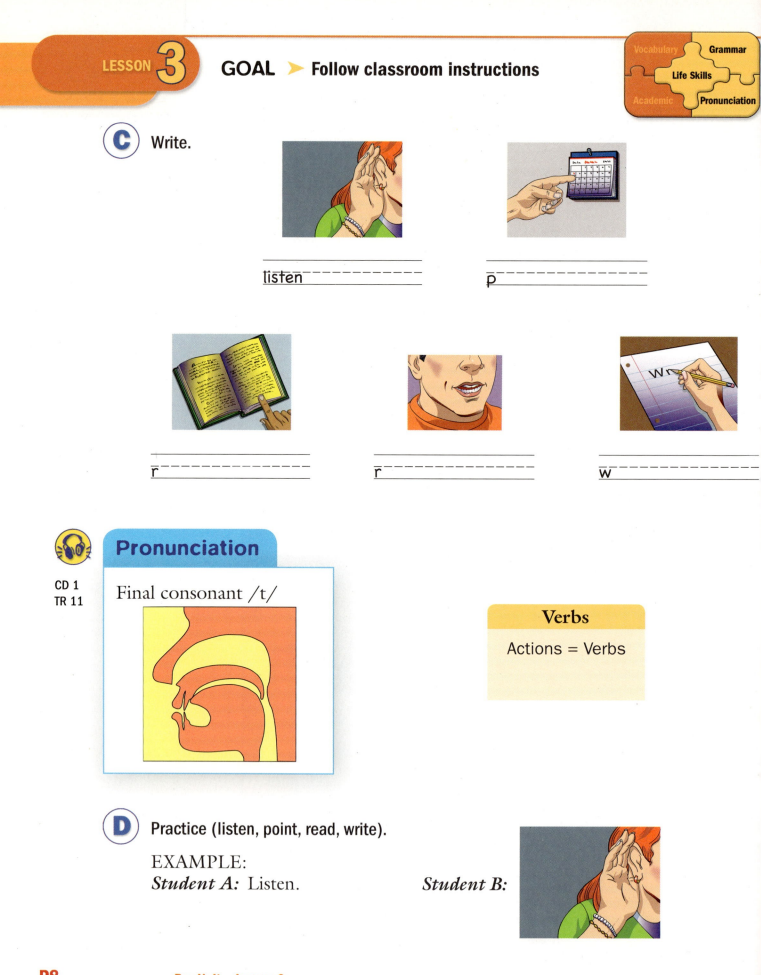

listen

p_____

r_____

r_____

w_____

CD 1
TR 11

Pronunciation

Final consonant /t/

Verbs

Actions = Verbs

D Practice (listen, point, read, write).

EXAMPLE:
Student A: Listen.

Student B:

LESSON 3

GOAL ➤ Follow classroom instructions

Vocabulary Grammar
Life Skills
Academic Pronunciation

E Read.

Circle.
1. pencil
   a. pen
   b. pencil
   c. paper

2. paper
   a. paper
   b. pen
   c. pencil

Bubble in.
3. pencil
   ○ pen
   ● pencil
   ○ paper

4. pen
   ● pen
   ○ paper
   ○ pencil

F Listen and circle the answers.

CD 1
TR 12

1.	2.	3.	4.
a. point	a. point	a. point	a. point
b. repeat	b. repeat	b. repeat	b. repeat
c. listen	c. listen	c. listen	c. listen
d. read	d. read	d. read	d. read
e. write	e. write	e. write	e. write

G Listen and bubble in the answers.

CD 1
TR 13

1.	2.	3.	4.
○ point	○ point	○ point	○ point
○ repeat	○ repeat	○ repeat	○ repeat
○ listen	○ listen	○ listen	○ listen
○ read	○ read	○ read	○ read
○ write	○ write	○ write	○ write

H Follow the instructions.

1. Circle the phone number. 02219   (212) 555-7763   04/08/09

2. Bubble in the answer. $2 + 2 =$ _____   ○ 3   ○ 5   ○ 4

3. Write the name of your teacher. _____

My Dictionary

Make flash cards to improve your vocabulary.

1. Choose four new words from this unit.
2. Write each word on an index card or on a piece of paper.
3. On the back of the card or paper, draw a picture of the word, find and write a sentence from the book with the word, and write the page number.
4. Study the words.

phone

Chinh's phone number is (714) 555-3450
page P6

Learner Log

Write the page number(s).

	Page Number	I can do it. ✓
1. Say: *I'm* (your name).	_____	_____
2. Say: *hello, hi, goodbye, bye.*	_____	_____
3. Say and write phone numbers.	_____	_____
4. Follow instructions.	_____	_____

Personal Information

GOALS

➤ **Identify classmates**
➤ **Express nationalities**
➤ **Express marital status**

➤ **Say and write your address**
➤ **Say and write dates**

LESSON 1

What's your name?

GOAL ➤ **Identify classmates**

CD 1
TR 14

A Listen and point.

What's his name?

He is a student.

What's her name?

She is a student.

What are their names?

They are students.

What's your name?

I am a student.

B Ask a partner the questions above.

EXAMPLE: *A:* What's his name?
B: He is Amal. He is a student.

GOAL ➤ **Identify classmates**

Vocabulary | Grammar
Life Skills
Academic | Pronunciation

C Listen and repeat.

CD 1
TR 15

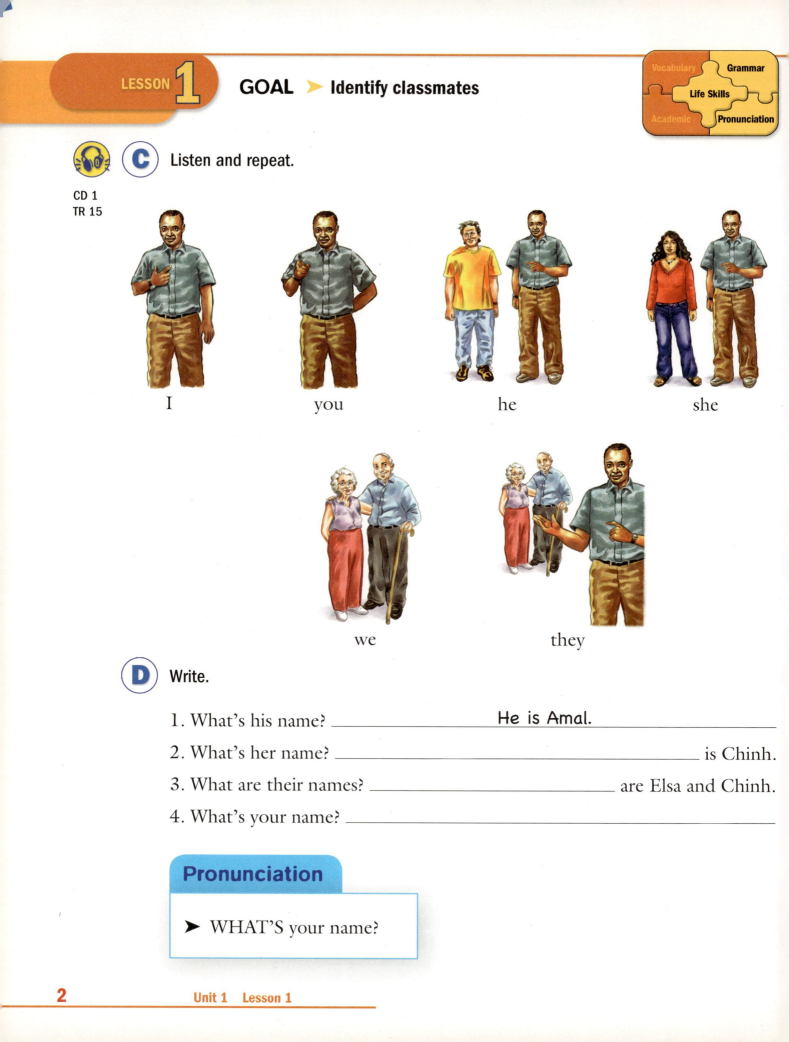

I   you   he   she

we   they

D Write.

1. What's his name? _____ He is Amal. _____

2. What's her name? _____ is Chinh.

3. What are their names? _____ are Elsa and Chinh.

4. What's your name? _____

Pronunciation

➤ WHAT'S your name?

GOAL ➤ **Identify classmates**

  E Listen.

CD 1
TR 16

Chinh: Hi, Satsuki.
Satsuki: Hello, Chinh.
Chinh: Elsa, this is Satsuki. He is a student.
Elsa: Hello, Satsuki. I am a student, too.
Satsuki: Nice to meet you.

F Practice the conversation.

G Work with a partner. Write classmates' names.

Pronoun		Name
I	I am a student.	(your name)
you	You are a student.	(your partner's name)
he	He is a student.	
she	She is a student.	
we	We are students.	
they	They are students.	

Where are you from?

GOAL ➤ Express nationality

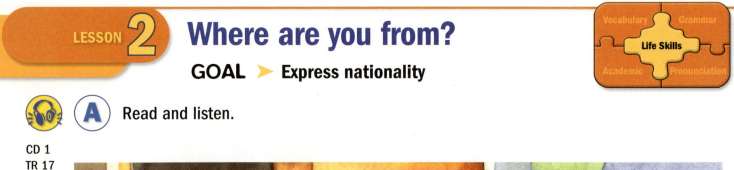

A Read and listen.

CD 1
TR 17

B Write.

1. What's her name? _____

2. Where is she from? _____

C Ask your classmates.

1. What's your name?

2. Where are you from?

LESSON 2

GOAL ➤ Express nationality

D Predict.

1. Where is Shiro from? _____

2. Where is Amal from? _____

3. Where is Chinh from? _____

4. Where is Elsa from? _____

E Listen and write.

CD 1
TR 18-22

1. She is from Cuba. _____Concepción_____

2. He is from Lebanon. _____

3. She is from Vietnam. _____

4. She is from Russia. _____

5. He is from Japan. _____

> **Birthplace**
>
> Where is he from?
>   He is from Japan.
>
> What's *his* birthplace?
> Japan.
>
> What's *her* birthplace?
> Cuba.

F Practice.

EXAMPLE: *A:* Where is <u>Concepción</u> from?   *A:* What's her birthplace?
           B: She is from <u>Cuba</u>.   *B:* <u>Cuba</u>.

GOAL ➤ Express nationality

Vocabulary Grammar
Life Skills
Academic Pronunciation

G Read.

Simple Present		
I	live	in Los Angeles.
He	lives	in Fort Lauderdale.
She		in Chicago.

H Complete the sentences.

1. Concepción ____is from Cuba____. She ____lives____ in Fort Lauderdale.

2. Shiro _____. He _____ in Fort Lauderdale.

3. Amal _____. He _____ in Fort Lauderdale.

4. Elsa _____. She _____ in Fort Lauderdale.

5. Chinh _____. She _____ in Fort Lauderdale.

6. I am from _____. I _____.

I Listen and practice using Shiro, Amal, Elsa, and Chinh.

CD 1
TR 23

Mrs. Adams: Hi, Concepción. Where are you from?
Concepción: I'm from Cuba.
Mrs. Adams: Where do you live?
Concepción: I live in Fort Lauderdale, Florida.

J Practice and write. Ask your classmates.

You: Hi, _____. Where are you from?
Classmate: I'm from _____.
You: Where do you live?
Classmate: I live in _____.

Name (What's your name?)	Birthplace (Where are you from?)	Current City (Where do you live?)
1.		
2.		
3.		
4.		

LESSON 3 — Are you married?

GOAL ➤ Express marital status

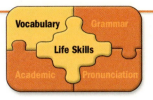

A Listen and write.

CD 1
TR 24

single   married   divorced

He is _____.

They are _____.

They are _____.

B With a partner, point at the pictures in Exercise A and say: *He is single, They are married,* or *They are divorced.*

GOAL ➤ **Express marital status**

C Read.

Be Verb			
Pronoun	**Be verb**	**Marital status**	**Example sentence**
I	am	married	I am married.
he	is	single	He is single. (Amal is single.)
she		divorced	She is divorced. (Mirna is divorced.)
we	are	divorced	We are divorced.
you		married	You are married.
they		single	They are single.

D Listen, circle *Yes* or *No*, and write.

CD 1
TR 25

1.

Is she married?   Yes   No

She _____ .

2.

Is he married?   Yes   No

He _____ .

3.

Are they married?   Yes   No

They _____ .

E Write *am*, *are*, or *is.*

1. Mr. and Mrs. Johnson ___are___ married.

2. Orlando _____ divorced.

3. Omar, Natalie, and Doug _____ single.

4. We _____ divorced.

5. They _____ single.

6. She _____ married.

7. We _____ single.

8. You _____ married.

GOAL ➤ **Express marital status**

F Read and write contractions.

I + am = I'm

You + are = You're

He + is = He's

She + is = She's

We + are = We're

They + are = They're

1. _____I'm_____ married.

2. _____ divorced.

3. _____ single.

4. _____ divorced.

5. _____ married.

6. _____ single.

G Write.

1. We ___are___ married.   We're married. _____

2. They _____ divorced.   _____

3. I _____ single.   _____

4. He _____ divorced.   _____

5. You _____ married.   _____

6. She _____ single.   _____

H Read.

A: Hans, are you single? | *A:* Lin, are you single? | *A:* Pam, are you married?

B: Yes, I'm single. | *B:* No, I'm married. | *B:* No, I'm divorced.

I Speak to five classmates.

Name	Marital status (Are you married?)
Hans	single
1.	
2.	
3.	
4.	
5.	

What's your address?

GOAL ▶ Say and write your address

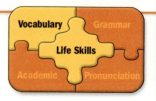

A Read.

Fawziya | Ahadi | 09-27-73
FIRST NAME | LAST NAME | BIRTH DATE

2687 Westpark Lane
STREET ADDRESS

Irvine | CA | 92714
CITY | STATE | ZIP

B Listen and point to the addresses.

CD 1
TR 26

3259 Lincoln Street
51 Apple Avenue
12367 Elm Road

C Write.

First Name: <u>Fawziya</u>

Last Name: <u>Ahadi</u>

Street Address: _____

City: _____

State: _____

Zip Code: _____

GOAL ➤ **Say and write your address**

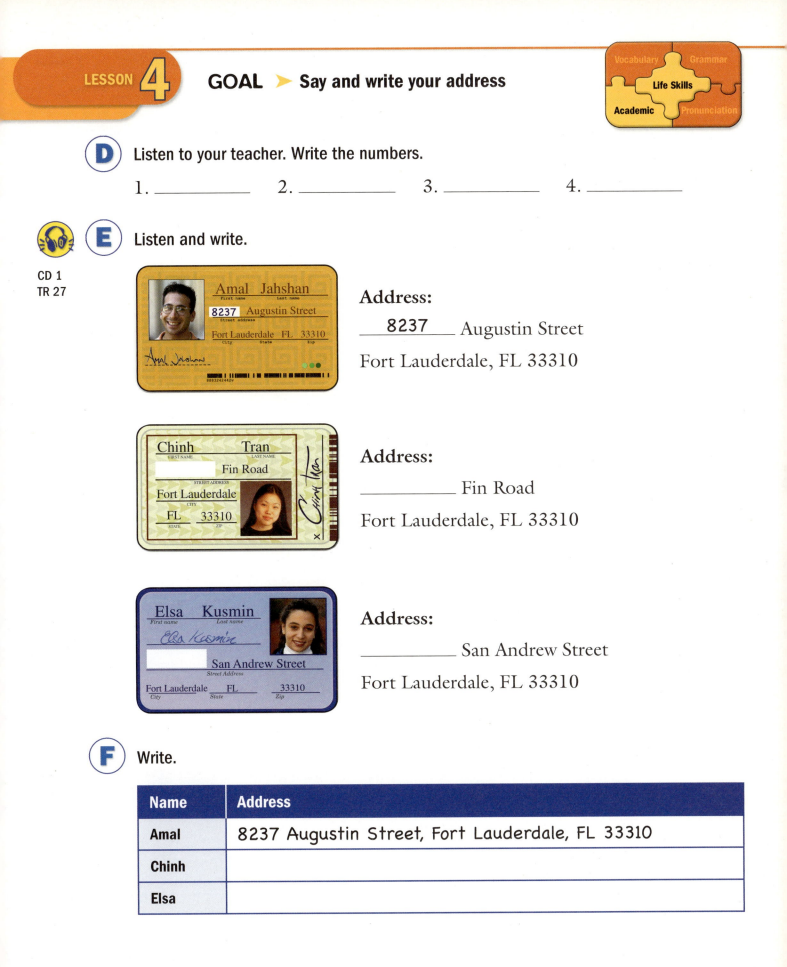

D Listen to your teacher. Write the numbers.

1. _____ 2. _____ 3. _____ 4. _____

CD 1
TR 27

E Listen and write.

Amal Jahshan
First name   Last name
8237 Augustin Street
Street address
Fort Lauderdale FL 33310
City   State   Zip

Address:

____8237____ Augustin Street

Fort Lauderdale, FL 33310

Chinh   Tran
FIRST NAME   LAST NAME
Fin Road
STREET ADDRESS
Fort Lauderdale
CITY
FL   33310
STATE   ZIP

Address:

_____ Fin Road

Fort Lauderdale, FL 33310

Elsa   Kusmin
First name   Last name
San Andrew Street
Street Address
Fort Lauderdale   FL   33310
City   State   Zip

Address:

_____ San Andrew Street

Fort Lauderdale, FL 33310

F Write.

Name	Address
Amal	8237 Augustin Street, Fort Lauderdale, FL 33310
Chinh	
Elsa	

GOAL ➤ **Say and write your address**

G Read.

Chinh: Hi, Amal. What's your address?
Amal: Hello, Chinh. My address is 8237 Augustin Street, Fort Lauderdale, Florida 33310.
Chinh: Thanks.

Be verb	
He	
She	
It	*is*
The address	

H Write.

Pair practice. Student A, look at page 12. Student B, look at page 11.

Student A: Hi, Chinh. What's your address?
Student B: Hello, Amal. My address is _____.
Student A: Thanks.

Student A: Hi, Elsa. What's your address?
Student B: Hello, Amal. My address is _____.
Student A: Thanks.

Student A: Hi, Amal. What's your address?
Student B: Hello, Elsa. My address is _____.
Student A: Thanks.

I Write.

My name	Address

My partner	Address

What's your birth date?

GOAL ➤ **Say and write dates**

Life Skills
Vocabulary Grammar Academic Pronunciation

A Circle this year. 2007 2008 2009 2010 2011

B Listen to your teacher and point.

09-17-2009

SEPTEMBER 2009						
Sunday	Monday	Tuesday	Wednesday	Thursday	Friday	Saturday
		1	2	3	4	5
6	7	8	9	10	11	12
13	14	15	16	17	18	19
20	21	22	23	24	25	26
27	28	29	30			

C Number the months.

January	February	March	April
01	_____	_____	_____

May	June	July	August
_____	_____	_____	_____

September	October	November	December
09	_____	_____	_____

D Listen to the months and say the number. Listen again and write the months on a sheet of paper.

CD 1
TR 28

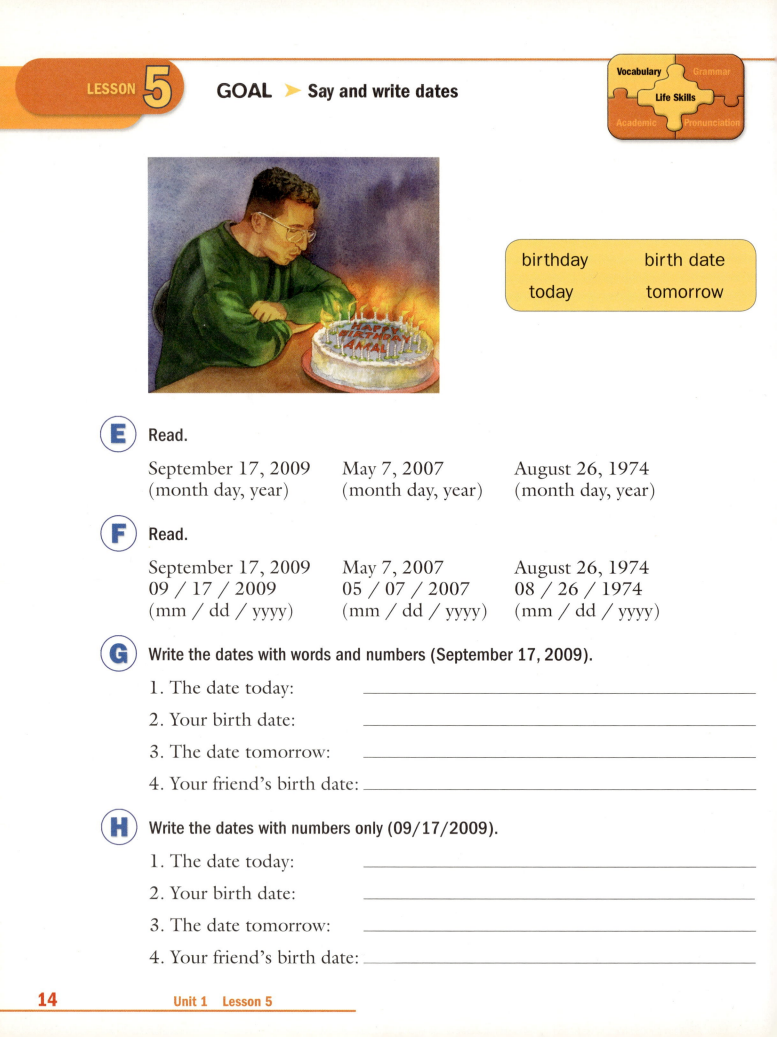

birthday   birth date

today   tomorrow

E Read.

September 17, 2009   May 7, 2007   August 26, 1974
(month day, year)   (month day, year)   (month day, year)

F Read.

September 17, 2009   May 7, 2007   August 26, 1974
09 / 17 / 2009   05 / 07 / 2007   08 / 26 / 1974
(mm / dd / yyyy)   (mm / dd / yyyy)   (mm / dd / yyyy)

G Write the dates with words and numbers (September 17, 2009).

1. The date today: _____

2. Your birth date: _____

3. The date tomorrow: _____

4. Your friend's birth date: _____

H Write the dates with numbers only (09/17/2009).

1. The date today: _____

2. Your birth date: _____

3. The date tomorrow: _____

4. Your friend's birth date: _____

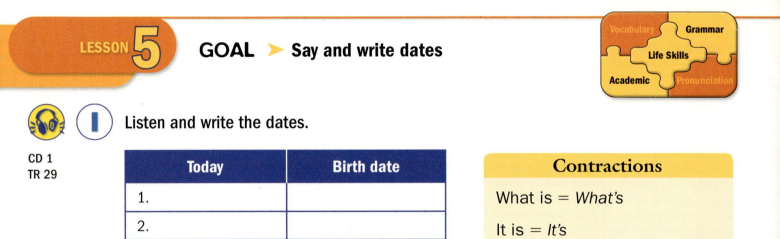

GOAL ➤ Say and write dates

Vocabulary | Grammar
Life Skills
Academic | Pronunciation

CD 1
TR 29

 I Listen and write the dates.

Today	Birth date
1.	
2.	
3.	

Contractions

What is = *What's*

It is = *It's*

J Read and practice with a partner using the dates from Exercise I.

Student A: What's the date today?
Student B: It's <u>June 25, 2008</u>.
Student A: Thanks.

Student A: What's your birth date?
Student B: It's <u>July 3, 1988</u>.
Student A: Thanks.

K Complete the calendar for this month and circle today.

Calendar

_____ (this month)

Sunday	Monday	Tuesday	Wednesday	Thursday	Friday	Saturday

L Write the date today. _____ _____, _____ or ____ / ____ / ____

Review

A Read. (Lessons 1–5)

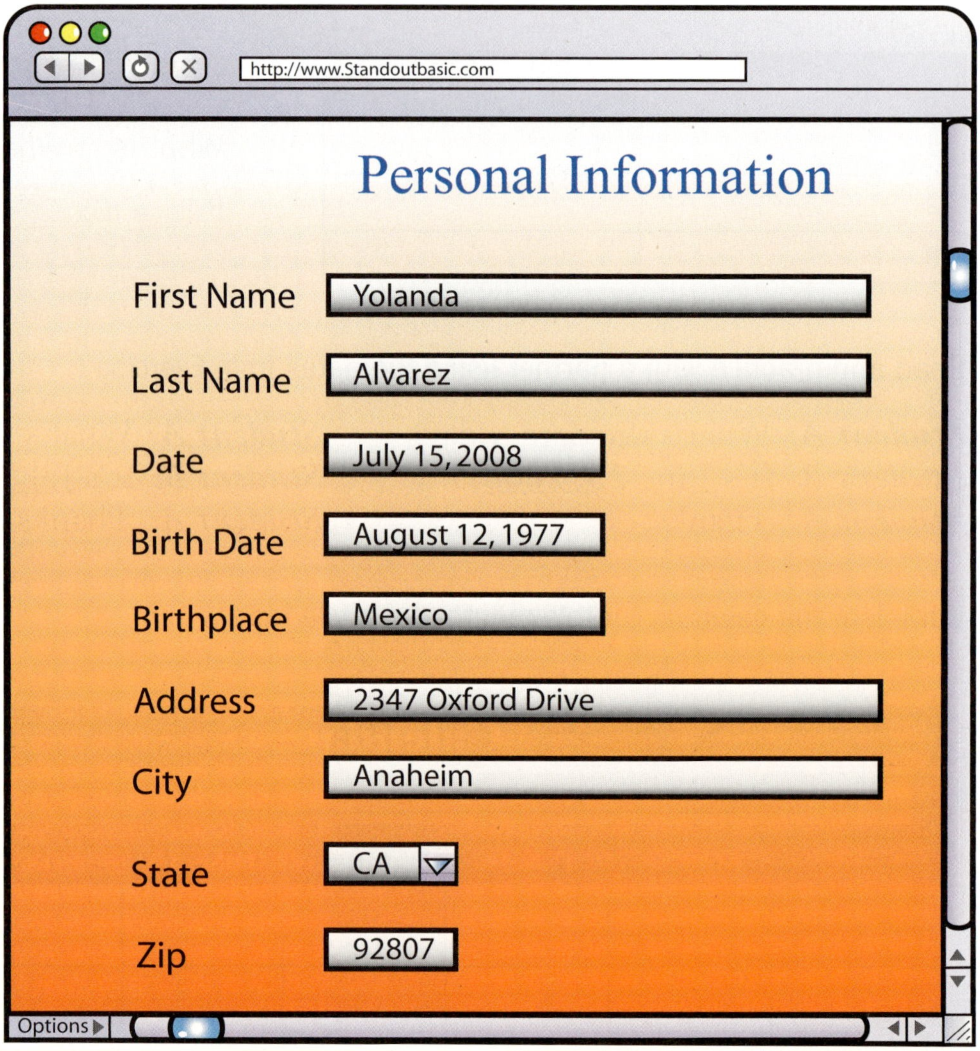

```
http://www.Standoutbasic.com
```

Personal Information

First Name	Yolanda
Last Name	Alvarez
Date	July 15, 2008
Birth Date	August 12, 1977
Birthplace	Mexico
Address	2347 Oxford Drive
City	Anaheim
State	CA
Zip	92807

Options ▶

B Write. (Lessons 1–5)

1. What's her first name? _____

2. What's her last name? _____

3. What's her address? _____

4. What's her birth date? _____

5. What's her birthplace? _____

C Speak to a partner. Write. (Lessons 1–4)

You ask: What's your first name?   What's your last name?
          What's your address?   What's your phone number?

Adult School Application

Last Name	First Name

Birth Date / / /	Birthplace

Street Address

City	State	Zip Code

Phone Number

D Match. (Lesson 3)

a.

1. single

b.

2. married

c.

3. divorced

Review

E Circle. (Lessons 1 and 2)

1.

She / He / They
is from Germany.

3.

She / He / They
is Ron Carter.

2.

She / He / They
are in school.

4.

She / He / We
live in Fort Lauderdale.

F Write the *be* verb. Then, write the sentence with a contraction. (Lesson 3)

1. She _____is_____ a student. _____She's a student._____

2. She _____ from Japan. _____

3. We _____ students at the Adult School. _____

4. They _____ from Honduras. _____

5. I _____ in school. _____

G Write *live* or *lives*. (Lesson 2)

1. He _____ in Portugal.

2. I _____ in Chicago.

3. She _____ in the United States.

My Dictionary

Make flash cards to improve your vocabulary.

1. Choose four new words from this unit.
2. Write each word on an index card or on a piece of paper.
3. On the back of the card or paper, draw a picture of the word, find and write a sentence from the book with the word, and write the page number.
4. Study the words.

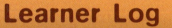
You are married.
page 8

Learner Log

Write the page number(s).

	Page Number	I can do it. ✓
1. *I / You / He / She / We / They*	_____	_____
2. Birthplace	_____	_____
3. *am / are / is*	_____	_____
4. *divorced / married / single*	_____	_____
5. Address	_____	_____
6. The date today	_____	_____
7. Birth date	_____	_____

My favorite page in this unit is _____.

Team Project

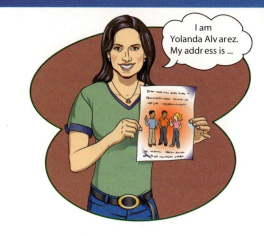

I am Yolanda Alvarez. My address is ...

Make a class book.

1. Form a team with four or five students. In your team, you need:

POSITION	JOB	STUDENT NAME
Student 1: Team Leader	See that everyone speaks English. See that everyone participates.	
Student 2: Writer	Write information.	
Student 3: Artist	Draw pictures.	
Students 4/5: Spokespeople	Organize presentation.	

2. Write the information for the members of your team.

   What's your first name?

   What's your last name?

   What's your address?

   What's your phone number?

   What's your birth date?

   What's your marital status? (Are you married?)

3. Draw a picture or add a photo of each member.

4. Make a team book.

5. Do a presentation about your team.

6. Make a class book with the other teams.

Our Class

GOALS
➤ Introduce your classmates
➤ Describe your classroom
➤ Identify classroom activities

➤ Tell time
➤ Describe weather

LESSON 1

Meet my friend.

GOAL ➤ Introduce your classmates

Vocabulary | Grammar
Life Skills
Academic | Pronunciation

A Look at the picture. Predict. Where are they from?

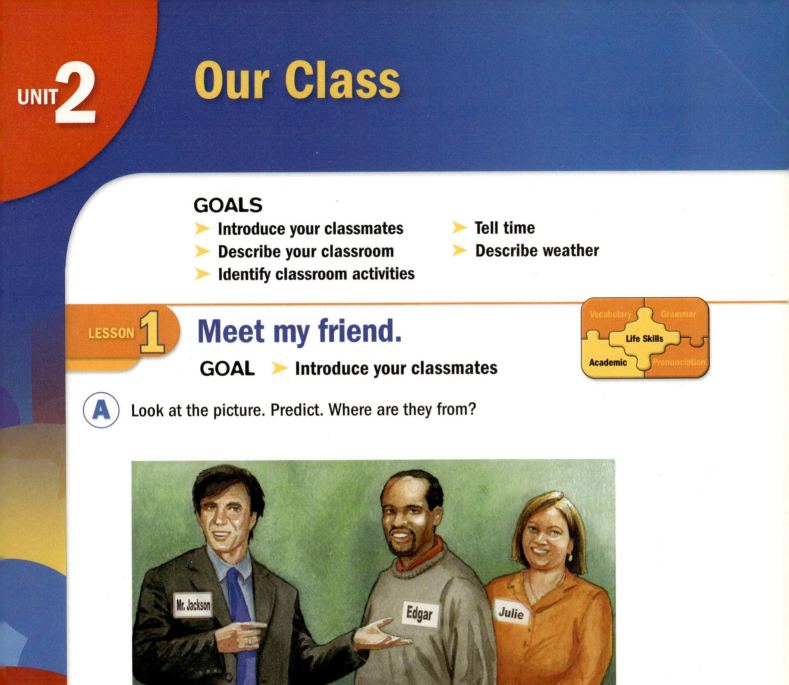

B Listen and practice.

CD 1
TR 30

I want to introduce two new students today. This is Edgar. He is from Senegal. He lives in Sacramento. His phone number is (916) 555-3765.

Meet Julie. She is also a new student. She is from Canada. She lives in Folsom. Her number is (916) 555-4565.

GOAL ➤ **Introduce your classmates**

 Read the chart.

Possessive Adjectives		
Subject	**Possessive adjective**	**Example sentence**
I	my	**My** phone number is 555-3456.
you	your	**Your** address is 2359 Maple Drive.
he	his	**His** name is Edgar.
she	her	**Her** name is Julie.
we	our	**Our** last name is Perez.
they	their	**Their** teacher is Mr. Jackson.

D Look at the pictures and complete the sentences.

This is Mr. Jackson.

_____ phone number is

555-2813. _____ address

is 3317 Maple Drive.

Irma and Edgar are married.

_____ phone number is

555-2350. _____ address

is 1700 Burns Avenue.

E Complete the sentences.

1. John is single. _____ address is 3215 Park Street.

2. You are a student here. _____ phone number is 555-2121, right?

3. We are from Russia. _____ address is 1652 Main Street.

4. I am a new student. _____ name is Julie.

GOAL ➤ **Introduce your classmates**

Vocabulary / Grammar / Life Skills / Academic / Pronunciation

F Learn the introductions.

This is …

Meet …

I want to introduce …

This is

This is Oscar.

This is Julie.

G Listen and circle.

CD 1
TR 31

1. This is   Meet   I want to introduce

2. This is   Meet   I want to introduce

3. This is   Meet   I want to introduce

Pronunciation

Emphasis

➤ WHAT'S your name?

➤ WHAT'S your address?

➤ WHAT'S your phone number?

H Talk to four classmates.

Name (What's your name?)	Phone number (What's your phone number?)	Address (What's your address?)
1.		
2.		
3.		
4.		

I Introduce a classmate to a group or to the class.

Where's the pencil sharpener?

GOAL ➤ Describe your classroom

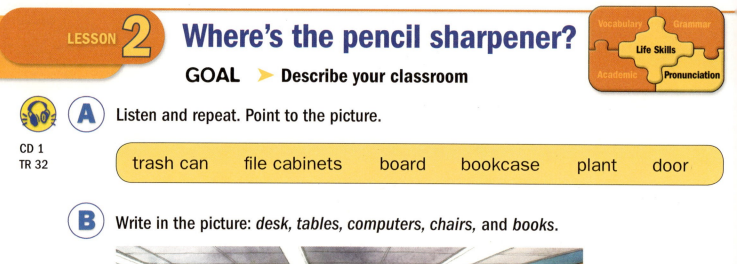

Vocabulary Grammar
Life Skills
Academic Pronunciation

A Listen and repeat. Point to the picture.

CD 1
TR 32

| trash can | file cabinets | board | bookcase | plant | door |

B Write in the picture: *desk, tables, computers, chairs,* and *books.*

C Listen and point.

CD 1
TR 33

Pronunciation

Emphasis

➤ WHERE'S the door?

➤ WHERE'S the trash can?

➤ WHERE'S the pencil sharpener?

D Ask questions and point. *Where's the <u>desk</u>? (trash can, board, bookcase, plant, door, pencil sharpener, computer)*

E Read.

Prepositions of Location	
	Where is the desk? It is **next to** the door.
	Where is the plant? It is **on** the desk.
	Where is the trash can? It is **between** the desk and the bookcase.

F Read.

Prepositions of Location	
	Where are the file cabinets? They are **in back of** the computers.
	Where are the students? They are **in front of** the board.
	Where are the books? They are **in** the bookcase.

G Ask *where is the* teacher, plant, and trash can. Ask *where are the* file cabinets, students, and books.

EXAMPLE: *A:* Where is the teacher?
            B: He is next to the door.

GOAL ➤ Describe your classroom

H In groups, draw your classroom.

I Write.

1. Where is the teacher's desk? _____

2. Where is the trash can? _____

3. Where is the board? _____

4. Where are the books? _____

5. Where are the file cabinets? _____

What are you doing?

GOAL ➤ Identify classroom activities

A Listen and point.

CD 1
TR 34

Shiro

Julie

Concepción

Edgar

B Write the names of the students.

1. listen   _____

2. read   _____

3. write   _____

4. talk   _____

| pen | pencil | book | notebook | CD | magazine | teacher |

C Write and match.

1.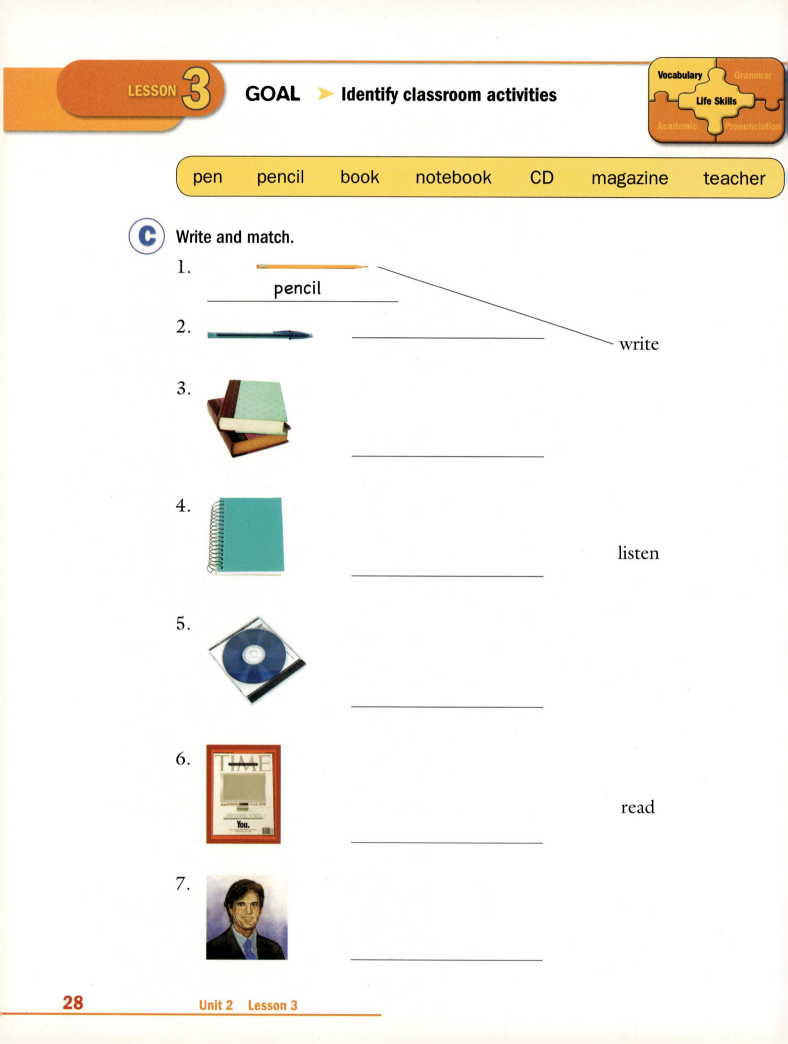

____pencil____

2. _____

3. _____

4. _____   listen

5. _____

6. _____   read

7. _____

write

GOAL ➤ Identify classroom activities

D Read.

Present Continuous	
He is reading.	She is reading.
He is writing.	She is writing.
He is listening.	She is listening.
He is talking.	She is talking.
He is sitting.	She is sitting.
He is standing.	She is standing.

She is standing.

She is sitting.

E Write.

1. She is reading.
2. She is listening.
3. He
4. He
5.
6.

F Write four sentences about your classmates.

EXAMPLE: Juan is sitting.

1.
2.
3.
4.

When is English class?

GOAL ➤ Tell time

Vocabulary | Grammar
Life Skills
Academic | Pronunciation

A Read and listen.

CD 1
TR 35

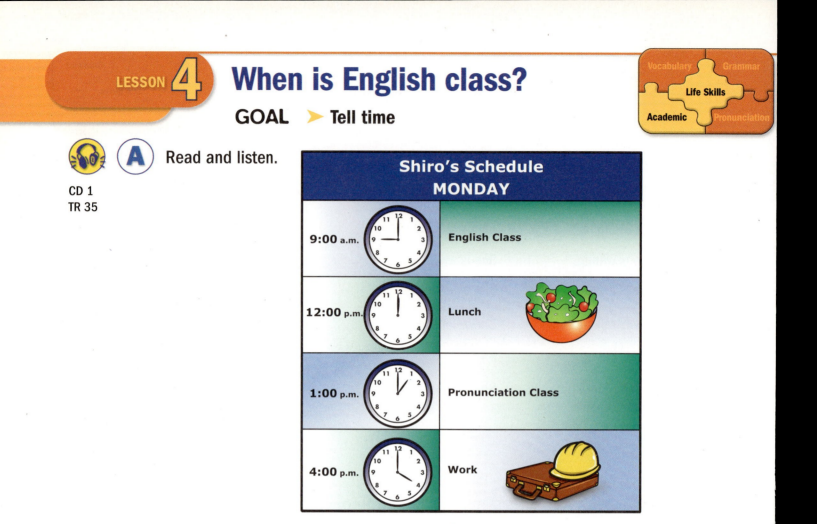

Shiro's Schedule
MONDAY

9:00 a.m.	English Class
12:00 p.m.	Lunch
1:00 p.m.	Pronunciation Class
4:00 p.m.	Work

Pronunciation

Emphasis

➤ WHEN'S English class?

➤ WHEN'S lunch?

➤ WHEN'S pronunciation class?

B Look at Shiro's schedule. Write.

1. When's English class? _____ It's at 9:00 A.M. _____

2. When's lunch? _____

3. When's pronunciation class? _____

4. When's work? _____

C What time is it now? Write.

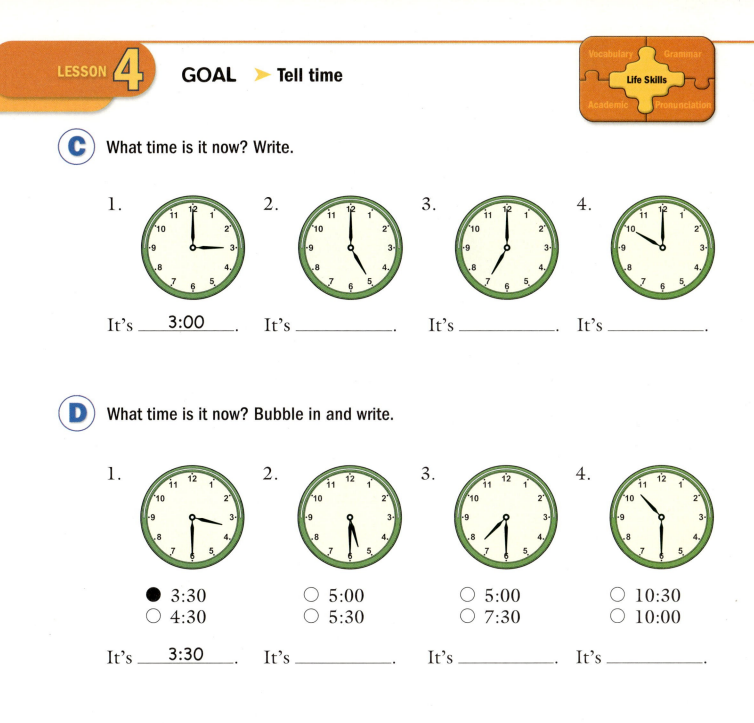

1.

It's ___3:00___.

2.

It's _____.

3.

It's _____.

4.

It's _____.

D What time is it now? Bubble in and write.

1.

● 3:30
○ 4:30

It's ___3:30___.

2.

○ 5:00
○ 5:30

It's _____.

3.

○ 5:00
○ 7:30

It's _____.

4.

○ 10:30
○ 10:00

It's _____.

E Point and practice.

EXAMPLE: *A:* (Point to Number 3 in Exercise D.) What time is it?
        B: It's 7:30.

GOAL ▶ **Tell Time**

Vocabulary   Grammar
Life Skills
Academic   **Pronunciation**

F Listen and write.

CD 1
TR 36

Julie's Schedule
MONDAY

9:00	English Class
_____	Work
_____	Lunch
_____	Bedtime

G Listen and read.

CD 1
TR 37

Julie: When's English class?
Mr. Jackson: It's at 9:00.
Julie: What time is it now?
Mr. Jackson: It's 7:30.

Pronunciation

➤ WHEN'S English class?
It's *at* 9:00.

➤ What TIME is it now?
It's *at* 7:30.

H Practice.

A: When's _____?

B: It's _____.

A: What time is it now?

B: It's _____.

I Write your schedule on another piece of paper.

LESSON 5

It's cold today.

GOAL ➤ Describe weather

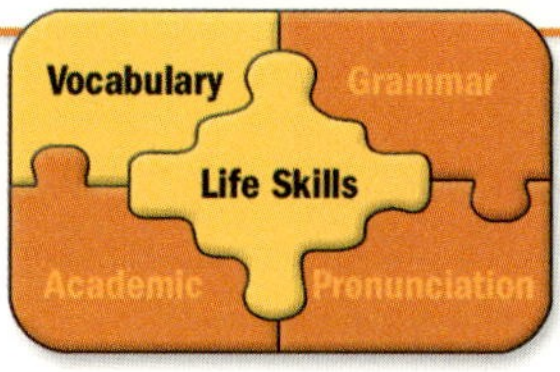
Vocabulary
Grammar
Life Skills
Academic
Pronunciation

A Listen and repeat.

CD 1
TR 38

windy cloudy foggy rainy snowy cold hot sunny

B Listen and write.

CD 1
TR 39

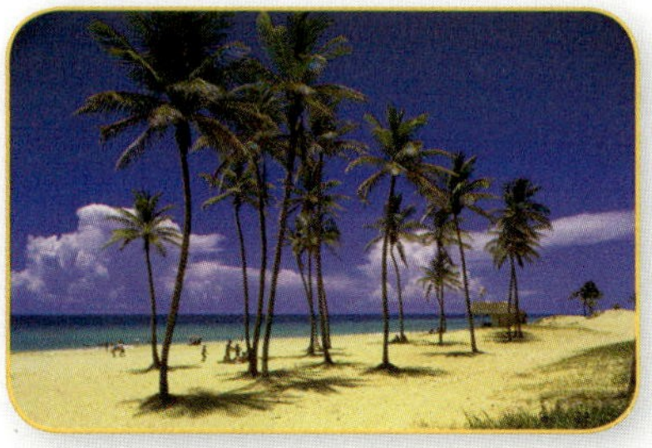

Havana, Cuba

hot

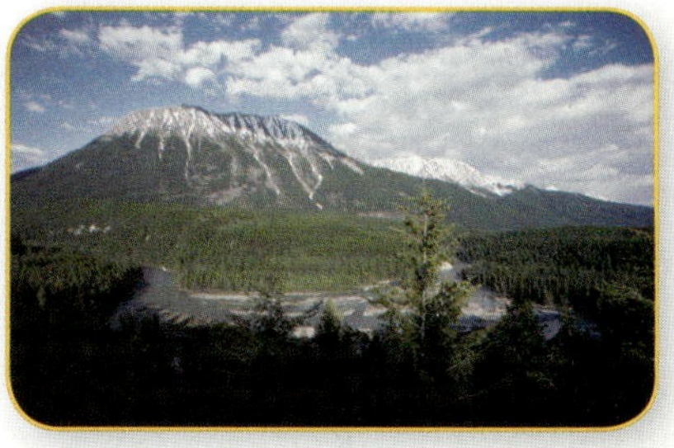

______

Montreal, Canada

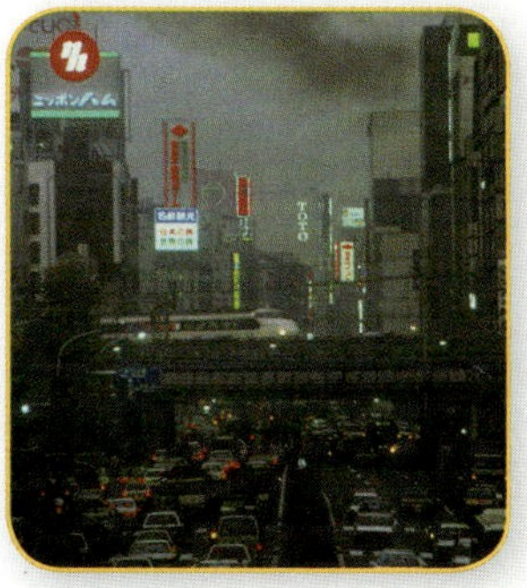

______

Tokyo, Japan

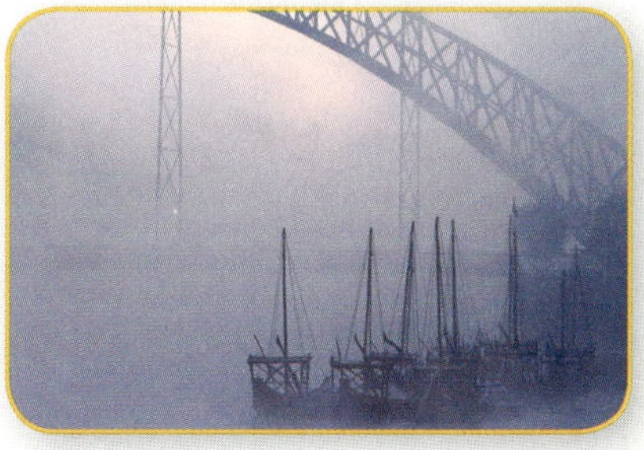

______

Lisbon, Portugal

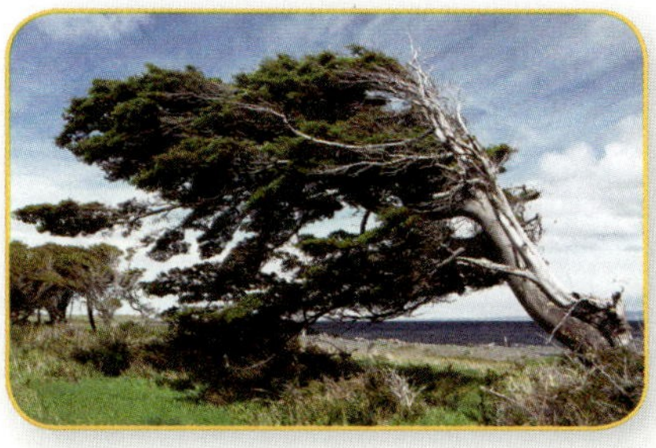

______

Patagonia, Chile

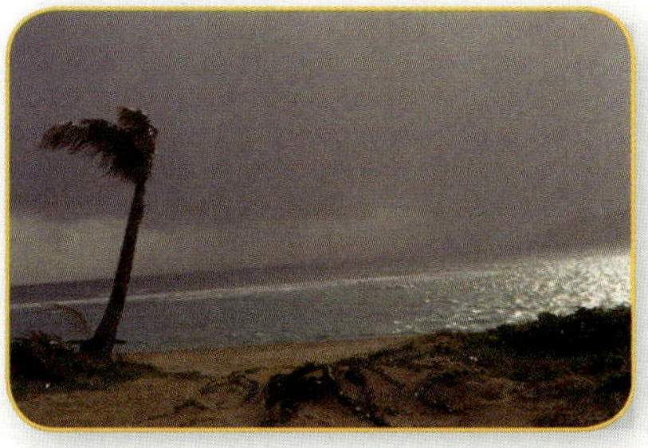

______

Mombasa, Kenya

  **LESSON 5** **GOAL ➤ Describe weather**

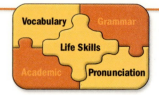

 C Review the weather.

Havana, Cuba

London, England

Capetown, South Africa

Moscow, Russia

Vancouver, Canada

Ensenada, Mexico

 Pronunciation

CD 1
TR 40

Emphasis
➤ HOW'S the weather in Havana?

D Read and practice.

A: How's the weather in Havana, Cuba today?
B: It's hot and sunny.

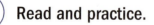

GOAL ➤ **Describe weather**

sandals   boots   a t-shirt   an umbrella

E Write the clothes above with the weather.

rainy   **sunny**

_____   _____

_____   _____

F Read.

Simple Present		
I, you, we, they	need	I **need** an umbrella.
he, she	needs	She **needs** an umbrella.

G Practice with *I, you, he, she, we,* and *they*.

A: How's the weather today?   *A:* How's the weather today?
B: It's rainy.   *B:* It's sunny.
A: He needs an umbrella.   *A:* I need a t-shirt.

H In a group, predict the weather for the week. Write *sunny, windy, cloudy,* etc.

Monday	Tuesday	Wednesday	Thursday	Friday	Saturday	Sunday

I **Active Task.** Go to the Internet or look in the newspaper. How is the weather in your home country today?

A Read. (Lesson 1)

1.

Application

Name
Choi Soon Young

Country of Origin
South Korea

Address
2237 Oakhave St.

City
Sacramento

State
CA

Zip Code
94203

Phone Number
916-555-7562

2.

Application

Names
Binh and Anh Duong

Country of Origin
South Vietnam

Address
4471 Broadway

City
Sacramento

State
CA

Zip Code
94203

Phone Number
916-555-3765

B Complete. (Lesson 1)

1. This is Choi Soon. He is from _____. _____ address is _____. _____ phone number is _____.

2. I want to introduce _____ and _____. They are from _____. _____ address is _____. _____ phone number is _____.

C Ask a classmate for information. Introduce your classmate to another student. (Lesson 1)

D Read. (Lessons 4 and 5)

Seoul, Korea   Guadalajara, Mexico

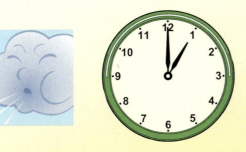 

Roanne, France   Lao Cai, Vietnam

E Write. (Lessons 4 and 5)

1. How's the weather in Korea? ___It's rainy in Korea.___

   What time is it? ___It's 8:00.___

2. How's the weather in France? _____

   What time is it? _____

3. How's the weather in Mexico? _____

   What time is it? _____

4. How's the weather in Vietnam? _____

   What time is it? _____

F Write. (Lesson 4)

It's 3:30. _____. _____. _____.

G Match. Draw a line. (Lesson 3)

1.

2.

3.

4.

a. He is listening.

b. He is writing.

c. She is talking.

d. He is reading.

H Write. (Lesson 2)

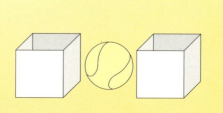 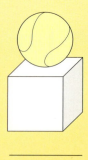

in _____ _____ _____

My Dictionary

Make flash cards to improve your vocabulary.

1. Choose four new words from this unit.
2. Write each word on an index card or on a piece of paper.
3. On the back of the card or paper, draw a picture, find and write a sentence from the book with the word, and write the page number.
4. Study the words.

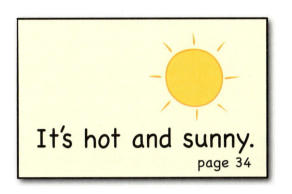

It's hot and sunny.
page 34

Learner Log

Write the page number(s).

	Page Number	I can do it. ✓
1. Introduce my classmates.	_____	_____
2. Describe my classroom.	_____	_____
3. Identify classroom activities.	_____	_____
4. Tell time.	_____	_____
5. Talk about the weather.	_____	_____

My favorite page in this unit is _____.

Team Project

Make a display.

1. Form a team with four or five students.
   In your team, you need:

POSITION	JOB	STUDENT NAME
Student 1: Team Leader	See that everyone speaks English. See that everyone participates.	
Student 2: Writer	Help team members write.	
Student 3: Artist	Arrange a display with help from the team.	
Students 4/5: Spokespeople	Prepare a presentation.	

2. Draw information about you on the team sheet of paper.

   Draw a picture of yourself.

   Draw a map of your country.

   Draw a clock with the time in your country.

   Draw the weather in your country.

3. Present each student's work in your group to the class.

GOALS

➤ **Identify common foods**
➤ **Express hunger**
➤ **Express quantity**

➤ **Make a shopping list**
➤ **Express preferences**

LESSON 1

Let's eat!

GOAL ➤ **Identify common foods**

Vocabulary | Grammar
Life Skills
Academic | Pronunciation

A Listen.

CD 1
TR 41

FAIR OAKS ADULT SCHOOL CAFETERIA

Tuna Fish

Chicken

Ham

Turkey

What's the name of the school?
Where are they?

B Listen again and read. Practice with a *chicken sandwich*, a *tuna fish sandwich*, and a *ham sandwich*.

CD 1
TR 41

Andre: The food looks good!
Silvina: Yes, it does.
Andre: What are you eating?
Silvina: A <u>turkey sandwich</u>.

GOAL ➤ Identify common foods

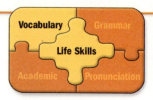

C Listen and point.

CD 1
TR 42

apples	butter	eggs	milk	tomatoes
bananas	cheese	lettuce	oranges	turkey
bread	chicken	mayonnaise	potatoes	water

D Write.

a. ___milk___   f. _____   k. _____

b. _____   g. _____   l. _____

c. _____   h. _____   m. _____

d. _____   i. _____   n. _____

e. _____   j. _____   o. _____

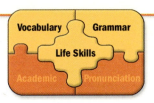
LESSON **1**

GOAL ➤ **Identify common foods**

E Read.

The potatoes are **in** the box.

The tomatoes are **on** the counter.

The oranges and apples are **over** the counter.

F Read the sentences and write the prepositions *(in, on, over, next to, between)*.

1. The water is _____ the milk.

2. The bananas are _____ the counter.

3. The turkey is _____ the bread and the cheese.

4. The milk is _____ the refrigerator.

5. The lettuce is _____ the counter.

G Practice. Use the sentences in Exercise F.

EXAMPLE: *A:* Where's the <u>milk?</u>
         B: It's <u>in the refrigerator</u>.

H What do you eat? Write.

Breakfast	Lunch	Dinner

I'm hungry!

GOAL ➤ **Express hunger**

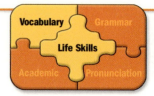

A Look at the picture.

Saul and Chen are studying English. What's for dinner?

B Listen and read.

CD 1
TR 43

Saul: I'm hungry.
Chen: Me, too.
Saul: What's for dinner?
Chen: chicken and vegetables

C Practice Exercise B.

What's for dinner?

a chicken
sandwich
and fruit

a hamburger and fries

a taco and chips

rice and
vegetables

GOAL ➤ Express hunger

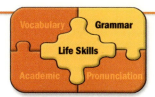

D Read.

Saul is hungry. He is not thirsty.

Chen is thirsty. He is not hungry.

Be Verb			
Subject	**Be**		**Example sentence**
I	am (not)		I **am** hungry. I**'m** hungry.
he	is (not)	hungry very hungry thirsty	He **is** hungry. He**'s** hungry.
she			She **is** hungry. She**'s** hungry.
we	are (not)		We **are** hungry. We**'re** hungry.
you			You **are** hungry. You**'re** hungry.
they			They **are** hungry. They**'re** hungry.

E Write. Follow the example sentences in the chart.

EXAMPLE: Edgar ____is____ hungry.
He's not thirsty.

1. Roselia and Thanh _____ thirsty.

_____

2. We _____ hungry.

_____

3. She _____ not hungry.

_____

4. I _____ thirsty.

_____

5. You _____ not hungry.

_____

GOAL ➤ Express hunger

F Read and listen.

CD 1
TR 44

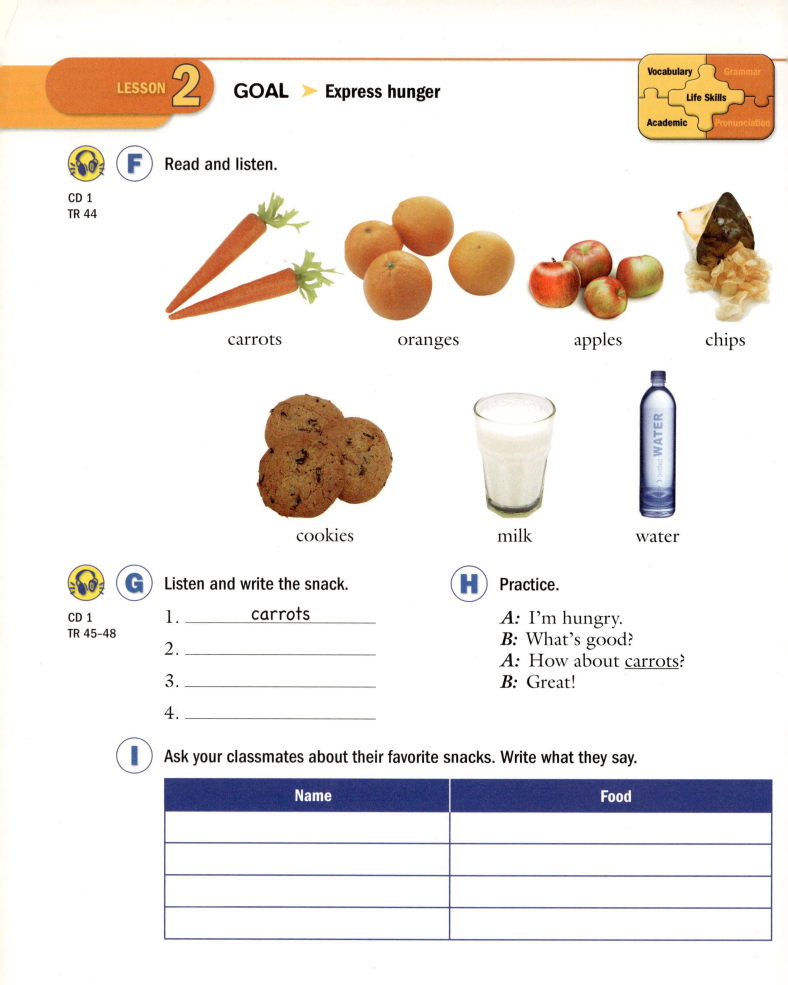

carrots   oranges   apples   chips

cookies   milk   water

G Listen and write the snack.

CD 1
TR 45–48

1. _____ carrots _____
2. _____
3. _____
4. _____

H Practice.

A: I'm hungry.
B: What's good?
A: How about <u>carrots</u>?
B: Great!

I Ask your classmates about their favorite snacks. Write what they say.

Name	Food

Let's have spaghetti.

GOAL ➤ Express quantity

Vocabulary | Grammar
Life Skills
Academic | Pronunciation

A Read the ingredients.

Spaghetti and Meatballs

Ingredients: Serves **6** people

Instructions:

Cook the pasta according to package directions.
Combine the eggs, chopped onions, salt, and pepper in a large bowl.
Add the beef and mix well.
Shape into 48

2 jars of tomato sauce	2 pounds of ground beef
2 eggs	salt
1 onion	pepper
1 package of spaghetti	

B Write.

1. How many jars of tomato sauce do you need? _____ 2 jars _____

2. How many eggs do you need? _____

3. How many onions do you need? _____

4. How many packages of spaghetti do you need? _____

5. How many pounds of ground beef do you need? _____

C Listen and circle.

CD 1
TR 49–52

1. jar   package   pound

2. jar   package   pound

3. jar   package   pound

4. jar   package   pound

GOAL ➤ Express quantity

D Read the chart. Listen. Repeat.

CD 1
TR 53

Singular and Plural Nouns	
Singular	**Plural**
jar	jars
can	cans
bag	bags
package	packages
pound	pounds
Exceptions: Singular potato tomato sandwich	**Plural** potato**es** tomato**es** sandwich**es**

E Write and say the plural forms to a partner.

EXAMPLE: *A:* What do you need?
               B: I need <u>apples</u>.

Pronunciation

Plurals

/s/	/z/	/iz/
chips	jars	packag**es**
carrots	cans	orang**es**

Fruit		Vegetables	
apple	/z/ apples	carrot	/s/
orange	/iz/	tomato	/z/
banana	/z/	potato	/z/
pear	/z/	pepper	/z/

GOAL ➤ Express quantity

F Write the words and the quantity.

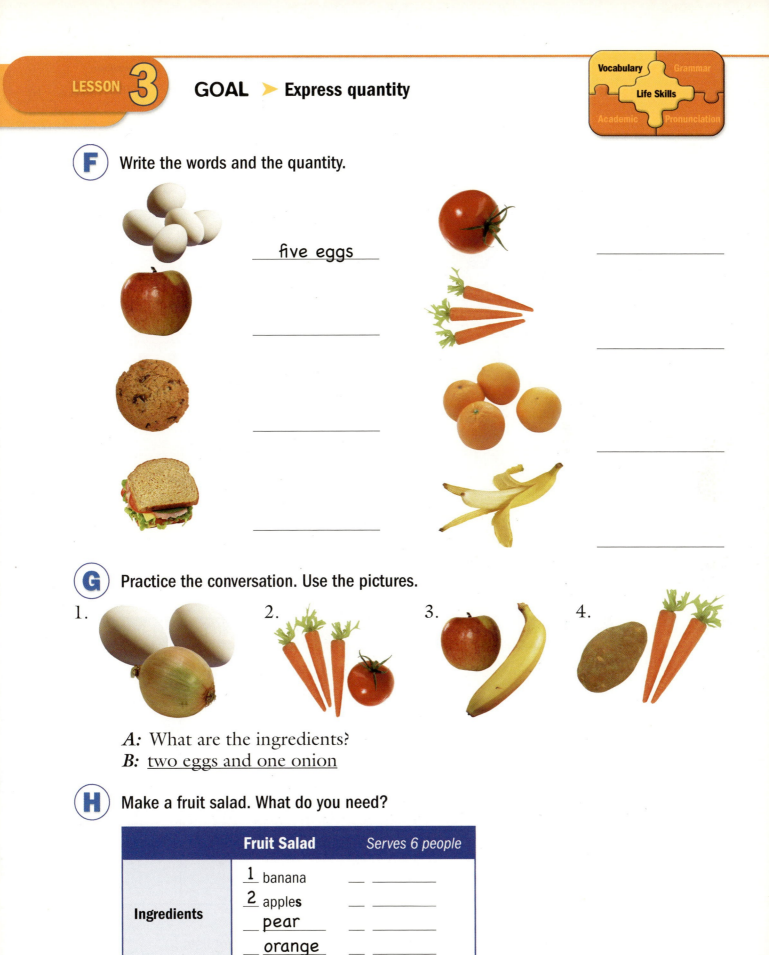

_____ five eggs _____

_____

_____

_____

_____

_____

_____

_____

G Practice the conversation. Use the pictures.

1. 2. 3. 4.

A: What are the ingredients?
B: two eggs and one onion

H Make a fruit salad. What do you need?

Fruit Salad		Serves 6 people
Ingredients	1 banana	__ _____
	2 apples	__ _____
	_ pear	__ _____
	_ orange	__ _____

What's for dinner?

GOAL ➤ Make a shopping list

Vocabulary · Grammar · Life Skills · Academic · Pronunciation

A Listen and point.

CD 1
TR 54

B Write the words on the correct shopping lists.

Shopping List	Shopping List	Shopping List	Shopping List
Meat and Fish	Vegetables	Fruit	Dairy
1. _____	1. _____	1. _____	1. _____
2. _____	2. _____	2. _____	2. _____
3. _____	3. _____	3. _____	_____
4. _____	4. _____	4. _____	_____
_____	5. _____	5. _____	_____
_____	_____	_____	_____
_____	_____	_____	_____

C Do you know more food words? Add them to the shopping lists.

GOAL ➤ **Make a shopping list**

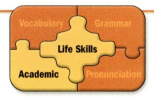

 D Read Amadeo's shopping list.

Shopping List

apples	tomatoes
water	chicken
milk	eggs
carrots	chips
cheese	

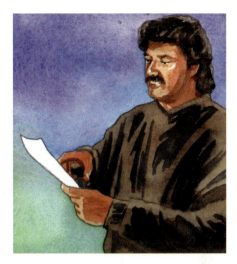

E What does Amadeo want? Circle the items.

oranges	potatoes
apples	cheese
eggs	broccoli

 F What does Yoshi want? Listen and write.

CD 1
TR 55

Shopping List

oranges _____   _____

_____   _____

_____   _____

_____   _____

_____   _____

GOAL ➤ **Make a shopping list**

Vocabulary   Grammar
Life Skills
Academic   Pronunciation

G Read.

Simple Present		
Subject	**Verb**	**Example sentence**
I, you, we, they	want	They **want** apples.
he, she	wants	She **wants** apples.
		He **wants** apples.

H Write and report. He wants ... She wants ... They want ...

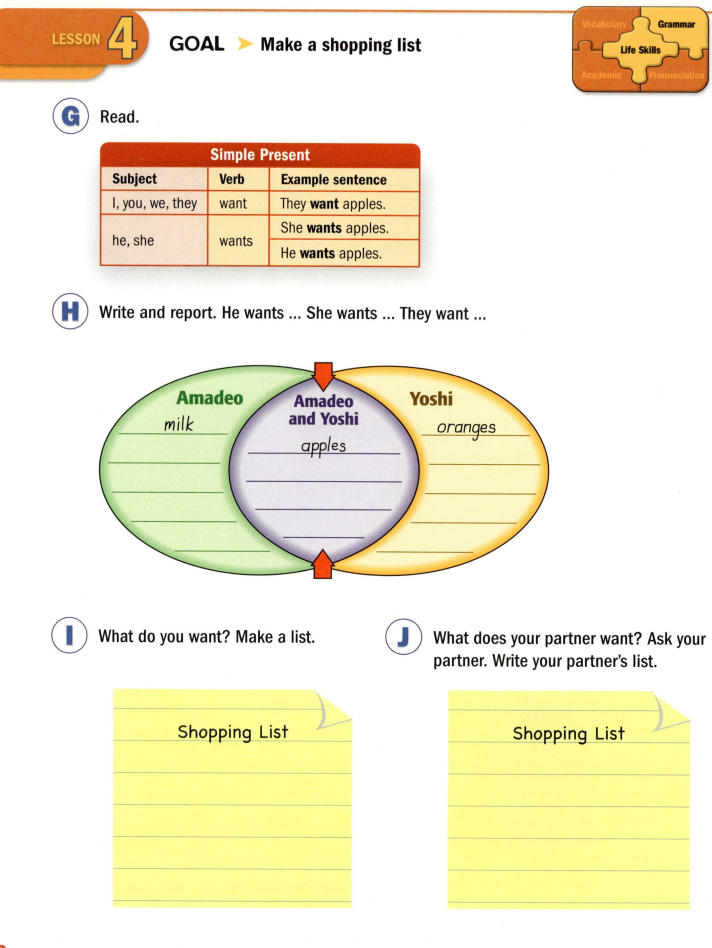

Amadeo
milk

Amadeo and Yoshi
apples

Yoshi
oranges

I What do you want? Make a list.

Shopping List

J What does your partner want? Ask your partner. Write your partner's list.

Shopping List

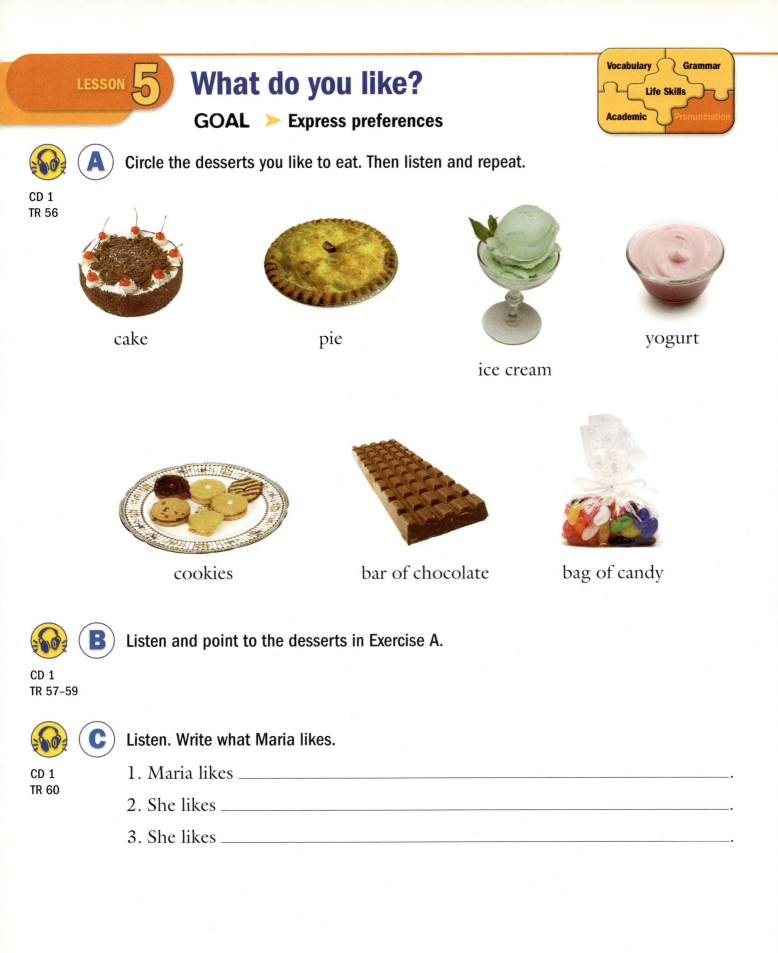

What do you like?

GOAL ➤ **Express preferences**

A Circle the desserts you like to eat. Then listen and repeat.

CD 1
TR 56

cake

pie

ice cream

yogurt

cookies

bar of chocolate

bag of candy

B Listen and point to the desserts in Exercise A.

CD 1
TR 57–59

C Listen. Write what Maria likes.

CD 1
TR 60

1. Maria likes _____.

2. She likes _____.

3. She likes _____.

GOAL ➤ Express preferences

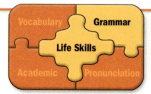

D Read the chart.

Simple Present		
Subject	**Verb**	**Example sentence**
I, you, we, they	like	I **like** ice cream.
	eat	We **eat** ice cream.
	want	They **want** ice cream.
he, she	likes	She **likes** chocolate.
	eats	He **eats** chocolate.
	wants	She **wants** chocolate.

E Write about the pictures.

      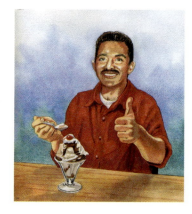

1. <u>He wants cookies.</u>   2. _____   3. _____

F Write the verb.

1. Maria ___likes___ (like) ice cream.

2. I _____ (want) apple pie.

3. You _____ (eat) pie.

4. They _____ (eat) cookies.

5. We _____ (like) fruit.

6. Saul _____ (like) candy.

7. We _____ (want) yogurt.

8. He _____ (want) cake.

9. We _____ (eat) chocolate.

10. They _____ (eat) candy.

11. Rhonda and Sue _____ (eat) pie.

12. I _____ (like) _____.

LESSON 5   **GOAL** ➤ Express preferences

 Read.

Student A: Do you like <u>ice cream</u> for dessert?
Student B: No, I like <u>pie</u>.

H Practice the conversation in Exercise G. Use all the words in Exercise A.

I Complete the diagram.

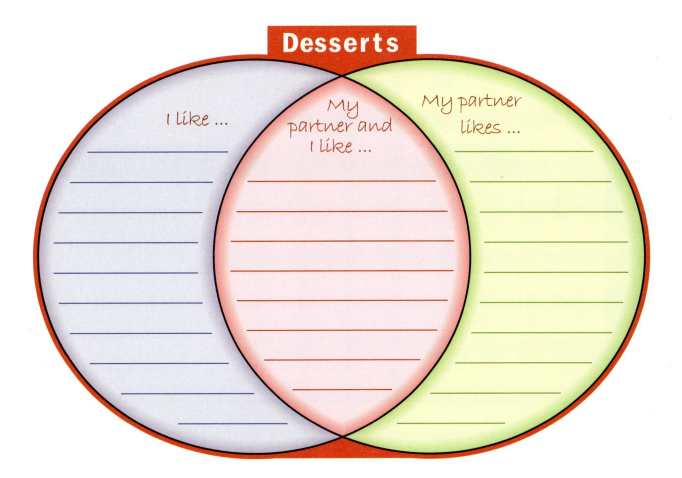

Review

A Write the food words. (Lessons 1–5)

_____ _____ _____ _____ _____

_____ _____ _____ _____ _____

B Write the plural food words. (Lesson 3)

Singular	Plural
apple	
orange	
chicken	
banana	
cookie	
egg	
chip	
potato	
tomato	
carrot	

C Write *am, is,* or *are.* (Lesson 2)

1. Maria _____ thirsty.

2. Kim and David _____ not hungry.

3. Lan and Mai _____ hungry.

4. Rafael _____ not thirsty.

5. Colby _____ hungry.

6. I _____.

D Write sentences. (Lesson 2)

EXAMPLE: Eric is hungry. ____He's not thirsty._____

1. Maria is thirsty. _____

2. Saul and Chen are hungry. _____

3. I am thirsty. _____

E Write the simple present. (Lessons 4–5)

1. Chrissy _____ (like) hamburgers.

2. You _____ (eat) tacos.

3. Laura _____ (want) vegetables.

4. Rosie and Amadeo _____ (like) rice.

5. We _____ (eat) fish and chicken.

6. I _____.

Review

F Talk to two classmates. Ask: *What do you want?* (Lesson 4)

Partner 1		Partner 2	
Shopping List		**Shopping List**	

G Read the lists in Exercise F. Write. (Lesson 3)

Singular Foods	Plural Foods

My Dictionary

Make flash cards to improve your vocabulary.

1. Choose four new words from this unit.
2. Write each word on an index card or on a piece of paper.
3. On the back of the index card or paper, draw a picture, find and write a sentence from the book with the word, and write the page number.
4. Study the words.

The water is next to the milk.

page 43

Learner Log

Write the page number(s).

	Page Number	I can do it. ✓
1. Identify common foods.	_____	_____
2. Express hunger.	_____	_____
3. Express quantity.	_____	_____
4. Make a shopping list.	_____	_____
5. Express preferences.	_____	_____

My favorite page in this unit is _____.

Team Project

Make a shopping list.

1. Form a team with four or five students.
   In your team, you need:

POSITION	JOB	STUDENT NAME
Student 1: Team Leader	See that everyone speaks English. See that everyone participates.	
Student 2: Writer	Write food names.	
Student 3: Artist	Draw pictures for the shopping list with help from the team.	
Students 4/5: Spokespeople	Prepare a presentation.	

2. You are a family. What is your last name?

3. Make a shopping list with food from this unit.

4. Draw pictures of the food on your list.

5. Present your list to the class.

Clothing

GOALS

➤ **Identify types of clothing**
➤ **Identify and find sections in a store**
➤ **Identify colors and describe clothing**

➤ **Make purchases and count money**
➤ **Read advertisements**

LESSON **1**

What's on sale?

GOAL ➤ **Identify types of clothing**

Vocabulary | Grammar
Life Skills
Academic | Pronunciation

ADEL'S CLOTHING EMPORIUM

Blouses Clearance **SALE!**

What's the name of the store?
What does Maria want?

a blouse

a shirt

pants

shoes

socks

CD 1
TR 61

A Listen.

Salesperson: May I help you?
Maria: Yes, I want a shirt, pants, a sweater, and shoes.

B Write three more sentences.

1. <u>She wants a shirt.</u>

2.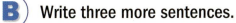

3. _____

4. _____

LESSON **1**

Vocabulary   Grammar
Life Skills
Academic   Pronunciation

GOAL ➤ Identify types of clothing

C   What's in the ad?

D   Listen and write the number of the conversation.

CD 1
TR 62

_____   _____   _____

_____   1   blouse   _____

_____   _____

E   Write the types of clothing in each picture in Exercise D.

GOAL ➤ **Identify types of clothing**

Vocabulary · Grammar · Life Skills · Academic · Pronunciation

F Read.

Simple Present: *Have*		
Subject	*Have*	**Example sentence**
I, you, we, they	have	I **have** two shirts.
he, she	has	She **has** a dress.

 Write.

EXAMPLE: (blouse) She _____has a blouse_____.
(shoes) He ____has shoes____. or He ___has a pair of shoes___.

1. (dress) She _____.

2. (coats) They _____.

3. (socks) I _____.

4. (sweaters) We _____.

5. (pants) You _____.

6. (shirt) He _____.

H What's in Maria's closet? Write.

Maria's Closet

3 _____

1 pair of _____

1 _____

 What's in your closet? Write.

My Closet

_____

_____

LESSON **2**

Where's the fitting room?

GOAL ➤ **Identify and find sections in a store**

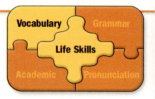

A Listen and point.

CD 1
TR 63

B Write the clothes you see in Exercise A.

Men's	Women's	Children's	Teen Boys'	Teen Girls'

GOAL ➤ **Identify and find sections in a store**

> Where's the women's section?

C Read.

Prepositions of Location

a. It's **in the front of** the store.

b. It's **in the corner of** the store.

c. It's **in the middle of** the store.

d. It's **in the back of** the store.

e. It's **on the left side of** the store.

f. It's **on the right side of** the store.

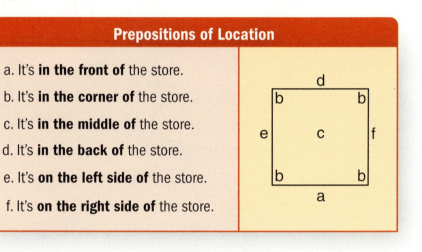

D Answer the questions. Look at page 64.

1. Where's the fitting room? It's in the back of the store.

2. Where's the men's section? _____

3. Where's the women's section? _____

4. Where's the children's section? _____

5. Where's the teen boys' section? _____

6. Where's the teen girls' section? _____

E Listen and practice. (Student A looks at Exercise D and Student B looks at page 64.)

CD 1
TR 64

A: Can you help me?
B: Sure. What can I do for you?
A: Where's the fitting room?
B: It's in the back of the store.
A: Thank you.

GOAL ➤ **Identify and find sections in a store**

CD 1
TR 65

F Listen and point.

CD 1
TR 66

G Listen and write the sections in the picture.

H In a group, write clothing in the picture for each section.

What colors do you like?

GOAL ➤ Identify colors and describe clothing

A Talk about the picture with your teacher.

What is Yusuf doing?
What color shirt do you like for Yusuf?

Pronunciation

Yes/No Questions

➤ Can I help you?

➤ May I help you?

➤ Do you need help?

 B Listen and read.

CD 1
TR 67

Salesperson: Can I help you?
Yusuf: Yes, I want a shirt.
Salesperson: What color do you like—white, blue, or red?
Yusuf: I don't know, maybe blue.

GOAL ➤ Identify colors and describe clothing

Vocabulary Grammar
Life Skills
Academic Pronunciation

C Listen and repeat.

CD 1
TR 68

red   yellow   blue

green   white   black

blue shirt (correct)

~~shirt blue~~ (not correct)

S = Small   M = Medium   L = Large   XL = Extra Large

D Listen and point to the clothing items.

CD 1
TR 69

E Look at Exercise D. Complete the chart.

Adel's Inventory List			
Quantity (How many?)	Item	Size	Color
	shirt	S	
2	shirt	M	
1	shirt		
2	shirt		

LESSON **3**

GOAL ➤ Identify colors and describe clothing

 Read.

Singular	Plural
There **is** one green shirt.	There **are** two black shirts.
There**'s** one green shirt.	

 Read and practice. Use the information in Exercise E.

A: How many <u>white</u> shirts are there?
B: There's <u>one</u>.

H Write an inventory for your class. Write about your classmates' clothing.

Class Inventory		
Quantity (How many?)	Item	Color

 Active Task. Go home and write an inventory of the clothes in your closet.

That's $5.00.

GOAL ➤ Make purchases and count money

A Listen and read the cash registers.

CD 1
TR 70

1.
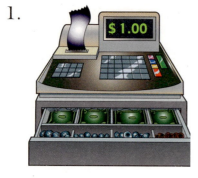

2.

3.

B Bubble in the number from Exercise A.

1. one dollar   1   2   3
                                          ○   ○   ○

2. ten dollars and forty-one cents   1   2   3
                                          ○   ○   ○

3. six dollars and twenty-five cents   1   2   3
                                          ○   ○   ○

C Practice the conversation with a partner.

A: How much is the <u>comb</u>?
B: It's $1.00.
A: Thanks.

GOAL ➤ **Make purchases and count money**

Vocabulary · Grammar · Life Skills · Academic · Pronunciation

D Listen and read with your teacher.

CD 1
TR 71

a dollar bill /
a dollar coin
$1.00

a quarter
$.25

a dime
$.10

a nickel
$.05

a penny
$.01

E Match.

a.

1. $.50

2. $15.08

b.

3. $35.10

c.

GOAL ➤ **Make purchases and count money**

Vocabulary · Grammar · Life Skills · Academic · Pronunciation

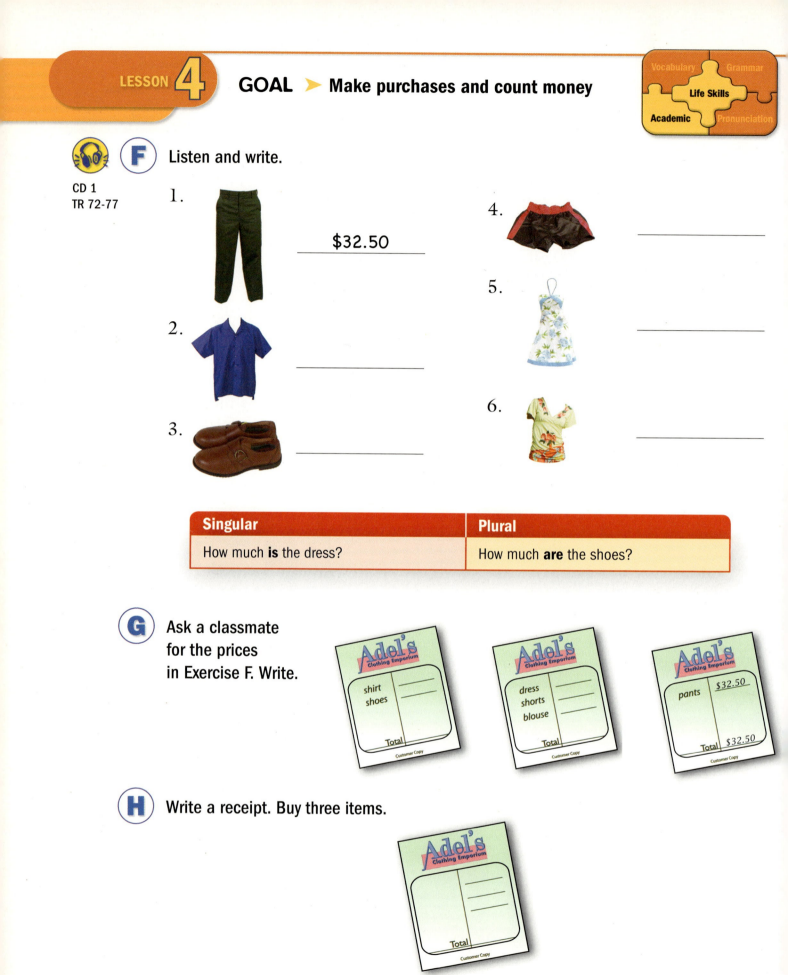

F Listen and write.

CD 1
TR 72-77

1. _____ $32.50

2. _____

3. _____

4. _____

5. _____

6. _____

Singular	Plural
How much **is** the dress?	How much **are** the shoes?

G Ask a classmate for the prices in Exercise F. Write.

Adel's Clothing Emporium
shirt _____
shoes _____
Total _____
Customer Copy

Adel's Clothing Emporium
dress _____
shorts _____
blouse _____
Total _____
Customer Copy

Adel's Clothing Emporium
pants $32.50
Total $32.50
Customer Copy

H Write a receipt. Buy three items.

Adel's Clothing Emporium
_____
_____
Total _____
Customer Copy

How much are the shoes?

GOAL ➤ Read advertisements

Vocabulary · Grammar · Life Skills · Academic · Pronunciation

A Read, listen, and write.

CD 1
TR 78

Save $5.00 · All Sizes · $22.50

Save $12.00 · Sizes 6-12 · _____

SALE · $33.00 · All Sizes

All Sizes · Save $4.00 · SALE · _____

SALE · All Sizes · $28.00

Save $5.00 · _____ · All Sizes

Adel's CLOTHING EMPORIUM

B Write.

1. How much are the shirts? __$22.50__

2. How much are the dresses? _____

3. How much are the shoes? _____

4. How much are the blouses? _____

C Ask a classmate the questions in Exercise B.

GOAL ➤ Read advertisements

D Read.

How much and How many		
Question		**Answer**
How much	(money) is the sweater?	It is $33.00.
How many	coats do you want?	I want three coats.

E Read and practice.

A: Can I help you?
B: Yes, I want some <u>shirts</u>.
A: How many shirts do you want?
B: I want two shirts. How much are they?
A: They are <u>$22.50</u> each.

> The sweaters are …
>
> They are …

F Practice taking orders from four classmates. Write. (Use the ad on page 73.)

Name	Quantity (How many?)	Product	Price
Yusuf	two	shirts	$22.50

GOAL ➤ **Read advertisements**

G   Read.

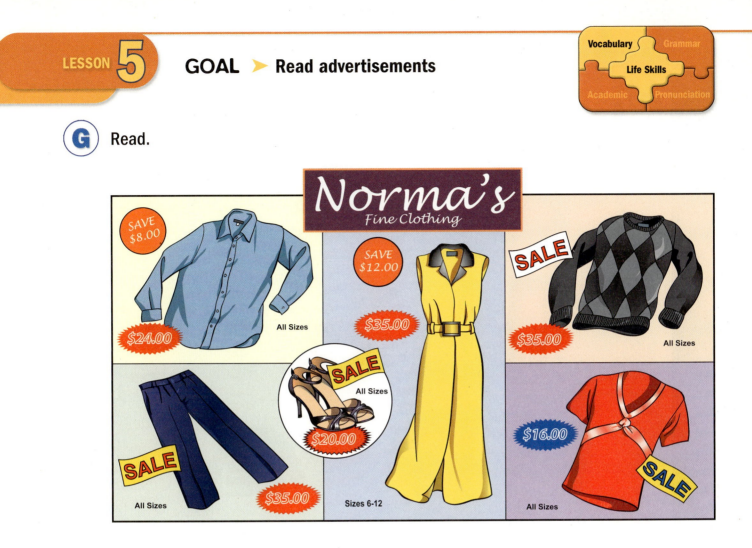

H   Compare Norma's Fine Clothing to Adel's Clothing Emporium (page 73). Write two receipts.

I   In a group, make an advertisement for a new clothing store. Practice the conversation from Exercise E.

Review

A Write the words. (Lesson 1)

1.

2.

3.

4.

5.

6.

7.

8.

B Read and write. (Lessons 3–5)

1. We need three blue shirts. They are $18.59 each.

2. We need five green sweaters. They are $22.50 each.

3. We need one pair of black shoes. They are $33.00 each.

4. We need two red coats. They are $85.00 each.

Adel's Clothing Emporium			
Quantity (How many?)	Item	Color	Price
1.			$55.77
2.			$112.50
3.			$33.00
4.			$170.00

C Write the locations. (Lesson 2)

a. It's in the corner of the store.

b. _____

c. _____

d. _____

e. _____

f. _____

D What money do you need? Write. (Lesson 4)

Total	$20 bills	$10 bills	$5 bills	$1 bills	quarters	dimes	nickels	pennies
$69.00								
$22.50	1			2	2			
$56.90								
$132.00								
$153.75								
$113.80								

E Read the ad. (Lesson 5)

F Write the information from the ad. (Lesson 5)

Item	Price	Savings
green pants	$28.50	$5.00
black pants		
white shirts		
blouses		
socks		
coats		

My Dictionary

Make flash cards to improve your vocabulary.

1. Choose four new words from this unit.
2. Write each word on an index card or on a piece of paper.
3. On the back of the index card or paper, draw a picture, find a sentence from the book with the word, and write the page number.
4. Study the words.

How much are the shoes?
page 73

Learner Log

Write the page number(s).

	Page Number	I can do it. ✓
1. Identify types of clothing.	_____	_____
2. Find sections in a store.	_____	_____
3. Describe clothing.	_____	_____
4. Count money.	_____	_____
5. Read advertisements.	_____	_____

My favorite page in this unit is _____.

Team Project

Open a clothing store!

1. Form a team with four or five
   students. In your team, you need:

POSITION	JOB	STUDENT NAME
Student 1: Team Leader	See that everyone speaks English. See that everyone participates.	
Student 2: Writer	Make an inventory list.	
Student 3: Artist	Make an ad for a clothing store.	
Students 4/5: Spokespeople	Prepare a presentation.	

2. Open a store. What is the name? Design the store.

3. Make an ad.

4. Write an inventory list.

5. Present your store to the class.

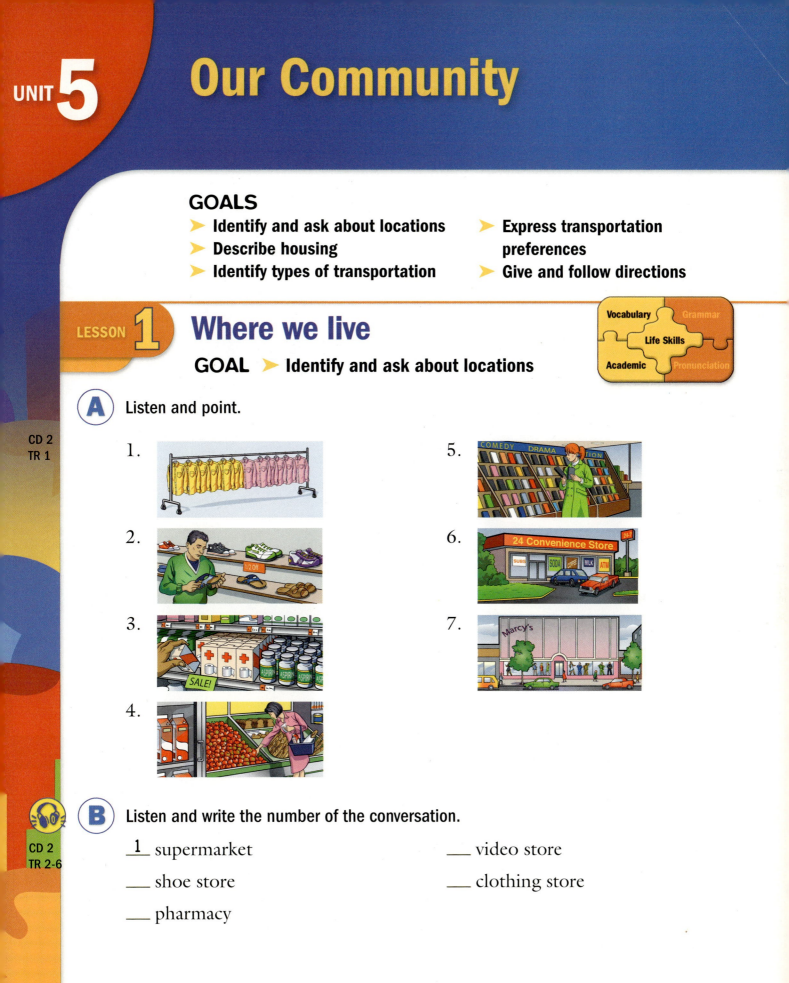

UNIT 5

Our Community

GOALS
➤ Identify and ask about locations
➤ Describe housing
➤ Identify types of transportation
➤ Express transportation preferences
➤ Give and follow directions

LESSON 1

Where we live

GOAL ➤ Identify and ask about locations

Vocabulary · Grammar · Life Skills · Academic · Pronunciation

A Listen and point.

CD 2
TR 1

1.

2.

3.

4.

5.

6.

7.

B Listen and write the number of the conversation.

CD 2
TR 2-6

_1_ supermarket

___ shoe store

___ pharmacy

___ video store

___ clothing store

GOAL ➤ **Identify and ask about locations**

C Listen and point to the signs.

CD 2
TR 7

D Write the places in Exercise C.

Place to sleep	Places to eat	Places to buy things
		clothing store

E **Read.**

Yes/No Questions	
Question	**Answer**
Do you buy clothing at a department store?	Yes, I do. No, I don't.
Do you buy food at a supermarket?	
Do you buy shoes at a shoe store?	

Pronunciation

Yes/No Questions

➤ Do you buy shoes at a shoe store?

➤ Do you buy food at a supermarket?

F **Practice with a partner. Ask about the places in Exercise A.**

A: Petcr, do you buy medicine at a pharmacy?
B: Yes, I do.
A: Which one?
B: Save-A-Lot Pharmacy.

> Which one? = Which store?

A: Maria, do you buy shoes at a shoe store?
B: No, I don't. I buy shoes at a department store.
A: Which one?
B: Marcy's.

G **Talk to four classmates. Write places they buy things.**

Name	Places
Peter	Jack's Supermarket, Rudolfo's Mexican Café

Where do you live?

GOAL ➤ **Describe housing**

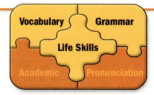

A Talk about the map.

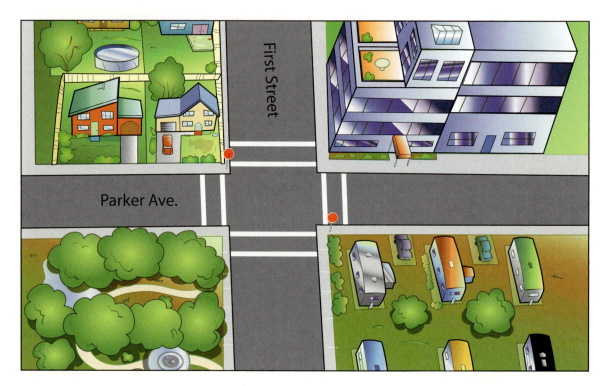

on / in
I live **on** First Street.
I live **in** a house.

a / an
a house
a mobile home
an apartment

B Listen and practice.

CD 2
TR 8

A: Where do you live?
B: I live on First Street.
A: Do you live in a house or an apartment?
B: I live in a house.

GOAL ➤ Describe housing

Vocabulary | Grammar
Life Skills
Academic | Pronunciation

C Read.

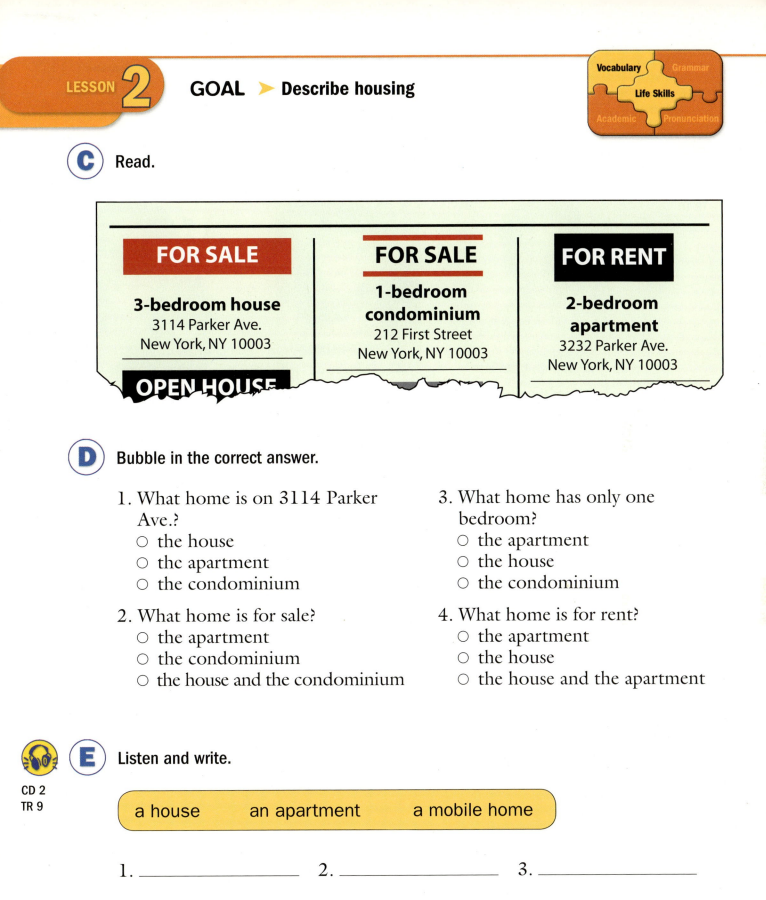

FOR SALE

3-bedroom house
3114 Parker Ave.
New York, NY 10003

OPEN HOUSE

FOR SALE

1-bedroom condominium
212 First Street
New York, NY 10003

FOR RENT

2-bedroom apartment
3232 Parker Ave.
New York, NY 10003

D Bubble in the correct answer.

1. What home is on 3114 Parker Ave.?
   ○ the house
   ○ the apartment
   ○ the condominium

2. What home is for sale?
   ○ the apartment
   ○ the condominium
   ○ the house and the condominium

3. What home has only one bedroom?
   ○ the apartment
   ○ the house
   ○ the condominium

4. What home is for rent?
   ○ the apartment
   ○ the house
   ○ the house and the apartment

E Listen and write.

CD 2
TR 9

a house   an apartment   a mobile home

1. _____ 2. _____ 3. _____

GOAL ➤ **Describe housing**

 F Listen and read.

CD 2
TR 10

1. I'm Chen.
   I'm from China.
   I live in a house.
   I live on First Street
   in Alpine City.

2. I'm Latifa.
   I'm from Saudi Arabia.
   I live in an apartment.
   I live in Casper Town
   on Parker Avenue.

3. I'm Natalia.
   I'm from Guatemala.
   I live in a condominium
   in Alpine City on
   First Street.

G Practice the conversation.

Chen: Hi, I'm Chen.
Latifa: Nice to meet you, Chen. I'm Latifa.
Chen: Where do you live?
Latifa: I live in Casper Town.
Chen: Do you live in an apartment, a condominium, or a house?
Latifa: I live in an apartment.

H Write a conversation.

Latifa: Hi, I'm Latifa.

Natalia: Nice to meet you, Latifa. I'm Natalia.

Latifa: _____

Natalia: _____

Latifa: _____

Natalia: _____

I Write and practice a conversation about you and a partner.

I take the bus.

GOAL ➤ **Identify types of transportation**

Vocabulary | Grammar
Life Skills
Academic | Pronunciation

A Look at the map.

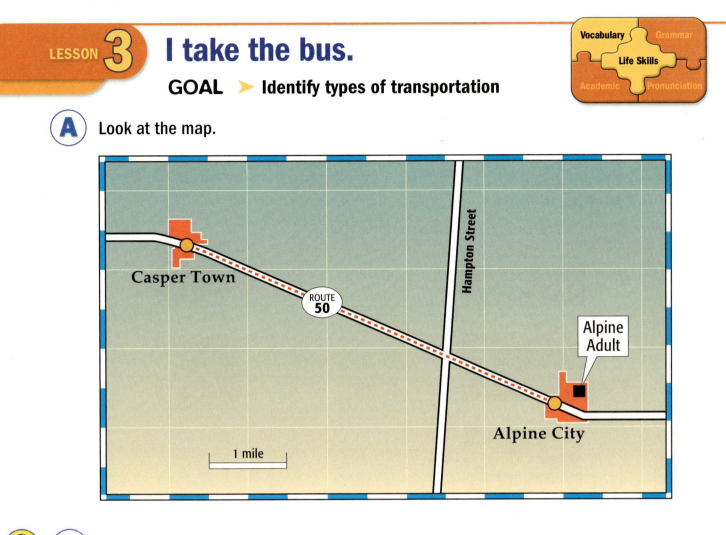

B Listen and read.

CD 2
TR 11

Chen: Do you drive to school?
Latifa: No, I don't. I take the bus.
Chen: How much is it?
Latifa: It's 75 cents.

C Ask four classmates.

Name	Do you drive or take the bus?

GOAL ➤ **Identify types of transportation**

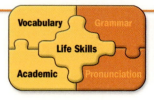

car	bicycle	taxi	train	bus

 D Write the words.

 _____car_____

 _____

_____

 _____

_____

 E Read the bar graph.

 F Ask a partner, *"How much?"*

EXAMPLE: How much is it to travel by bus?

GOAL ➤ **Identify types of transportation**

Vocabulary | Grammar
Life Skills
Academic | Pronunciation

G Read.

drive a car	take a bus
ride a bike	take a train
walk	take a taxi

Come and Go	
You are at school. You ask, "How do you **come** to school?"	You are at home. You ask, "How do you **go** to school?"
You are at school. You ask, "How do you **go** home?"	You are at home. You ask, "How do you **come** home?"

H Practice the conversation.

Latifa: How do you come to school?
Natalia: I drive.
Latifa: When do you go home?
Natalia: I go home at 3:00.

I Ask four classmates.

Name	How do you come to school?	When do you go home?
Natalia	drives	3:00

J **Active Task.** How much does the bus cost to go from your home to school? _____

She takes the train.

GOAL ➤ Express transportation preferences

A Listen and write.

CD 2
TR 12

1. I'm James.
I'm from the
United States.
I live in a house.

I take the _____
to school.

2. I'm Nga.
I'm from Vietnam.
I live in a house.

I _____ a bicycle
to school.

3. I'm Carina.
I'm from Cuba.
I live in an

_____.
I drive to school.

B Write.

Name	Country	Housing	Transportation
James			
Nga			
Carina			

GOAL ➤ Express transportation preferences

C Read.

Simple Present		
Subject	**Verb**	**Example sentence**
I, you, we, they	live	I **live** in Mexico.
	take	We **take** the bus.
	ride	You **ride** a bicycle.
	walk	They **take** a train.
he, she, it	live**s** takes**s** rides**s** walk**s**	He **takes** the bus. She **rides** a bicycle.

D Write about James, Carina, and Nga.

1. James _____lives_____ in a house.

2. He _____ the bus to school.

3. Carina _____ in an apartment.

4. She _____ to school.

5. Nga _____ in a house.

6. She _____ a bicycle to school.

7. James and Nga _____ in a house.

E Write about Leslie and Briana.

1. Leslie and Briana _____ in Cambodia.

2. Leslie _____ the bus to work every day.

3. Briana _____ a car to work.

4. They _____ in a house.

GOAL ➤ Express transportation preferences

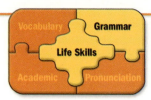

F Read.

Simple Present: *Be* Verb		
Subject	***Be* Verb**	**Example sentence**
I	am	I **am** Nga.
he, she, it	is	She **is** from China.
we, you, they	are	They **are** married.

G Read the chart.

Name	Country	Housing	Transportation to school
Karen	United States	house	bus
Sang	China	apartment	bus

H Write.

1. Karen _____is_____ from the United States.

2. Karen _____ in a house.

3. She _____ the bus.

4. Sang _____ from China.

5. He _____ in an apartment.

6. Karen and Sang _____ the bus.

I Answer the questions.

1. What's your name?

   My name _____.

2. Where are you from?

   I _____ from

   _____.

3. Do you live in a house?

   I _____ in a(n)

   _____.

4. How do you come to school?

   I _____ to school.

LESSON 5 — Where's the store?

GOAL ➤ Give and follow directions

Vocabulary
Grammar
Life Skills
Academic
Pronunciation

A Talk about the map of Alpine City.

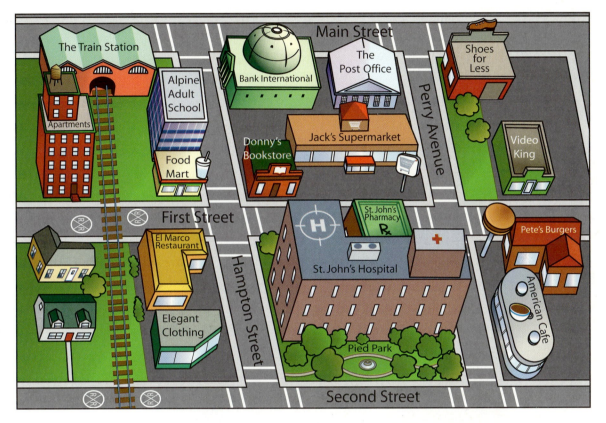

B Learn the new words.

> bank   post office   hospital

the
the post office
~~**the**~~ Shoes for Less
~~**the**~~ First Street

C Match. Draw a line.

1. Where is the adult school?
2. Where is the video store?
3. Where is the bookstore?
4. Where is the post office?

a. It's on Perry Avenue next to Shoes for Less.
b. It's on First Street next to the supermarket.
c. It's on Main Street next to the bank.
d. It's on Hampton Street next to Food Mart.

D Listen and repeat.

CD 2
TR 13

| stop | go straight | turn right | turn left |

E Write the correct words.

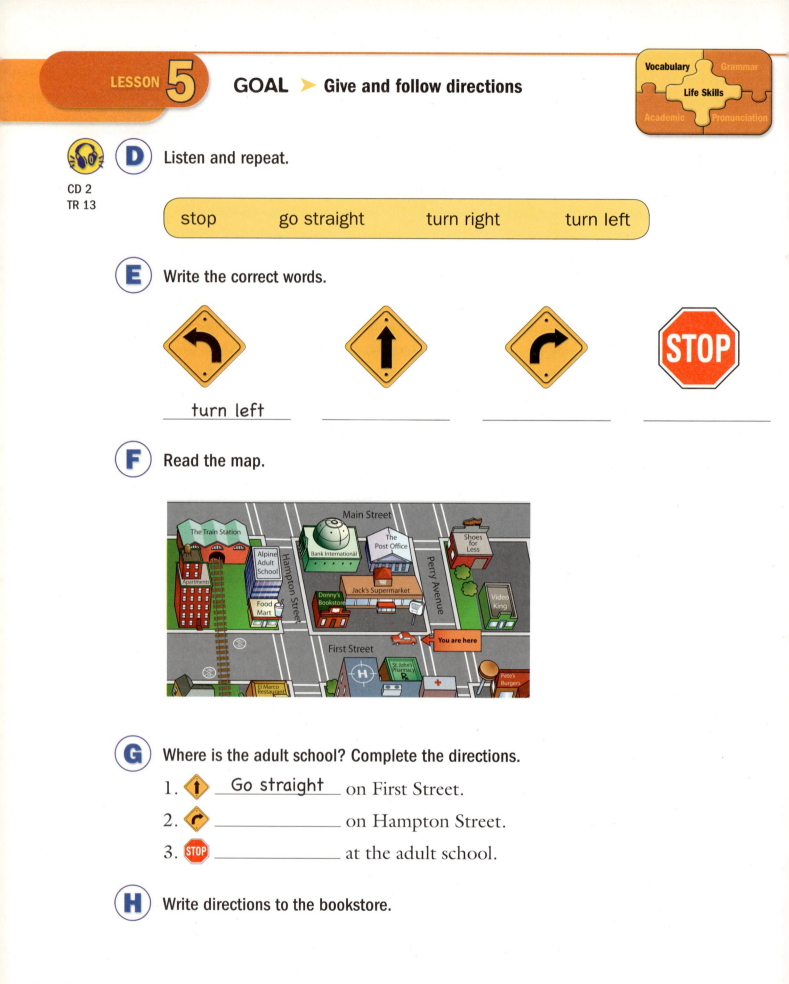

turn left   _____   _____   _____

F Read the map.

G Where is the adult school? Complete the directions.

1.   __Go straight__ on First Street.

2.   _____ on Hampton Street.

3.   _____ at the adult school.

H Write directions to the bookstore.

I Listen and read.

CD 2
TR 14

Carina: Excuse me, where's American Café?
Nga: It's on Perry Avenue.
Carina: Can you give me directions?
Nga: Yes. Go straight on First Street. Turn right on Perry Avenue. It's next to Pete's Burgers.

J Listen and follow the directions. Number the locations 1–4.

CD 2
TR 15

K Write three stores in your community.

1. _____   2. _____   3. _____

L Write directions to one store from your school.

_____

_____

_____

_____

Review

A) Write the correct letter. (Lessons 1–5)

1. __ apartment
2. __ bank
3. __ bus
4. _a_ car
5. __ hospital
6. __ house
7. __ pharmacy
8. __ stop sign
9. __ supermarket
10. __ taxi
11. __ train
12. __ turn left sign

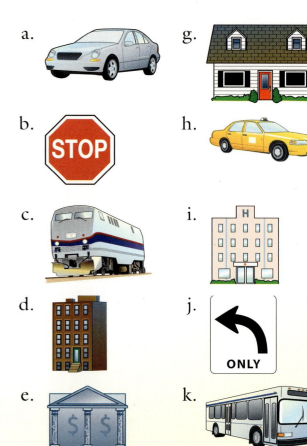

a.

b.

c.

d.

e.

f.

g.

h.

i.

j.

k.

l.

B) Practice with a partner. (Lesson 1)

1. Where do you live?
2. Where do you buy clothing?
3. Where do you buy shoes?
4. Where do you eat?

1. I'm Aki.
   I'm from Japan.
   I live in an apartment.
   I live in New York on
     Second Street.
   I drive to school.

2. I'm Adriano.
   I'm from Italy.
   I live in a house.
   I live in New York on Broadway.
   I take the bus to school.

C Write and practice a conversation. (Lessons 2 and 4)

Aki: Hi, Adriano. Where do you live? _____

Adriano: _____

Aki: _____

Adriano: _____

Aki: _____

Adriano: _____

D Write. (Lesson 4)

1. Aki _____ to school.

2. Adriano _____ to school.

3. They _____ in New York.

Review

 E Read the map. (Lesson 5)

Broadway Street

Train Station   Restaurant

Apartments

Pharmacy

Apartments

Shoe Store

Adult School

Nexus Street

Video Store

Fast Food

Restaurant

Olive Street

Post Office

Hospital

Supermarket

Women's Clothing

Men's Clothing

Bank

Standard Avenue

You are here

 F Write the place. (Lesson 5)

Place	Directions
the post office	Turn right on Nexus. Turn left on Main. It's next to the supermarket.
	Go straight. Turn right on Olive Street. It's next to the houses.
	Go straight. Turn right on Olive Street. Turn right on Main Street. It's next to the adult school.
	Turn right on Nexus. Turn left on Broadway. It's next to the restaurant.

My Dictionary

Make flash cards to improve your vocabulary.

1. Choose four new words from this unit.
2. Write each word on an index card or on a piece of paper.
3. On the back of the index card or paper, draw a picture, find and write a sentence from the book with the word, and write the page number.
4. Study the words.

I live in a condominium.
page 86

Learner Log

Write the page number(s).

	Page Number	I can do it. ✓
1. Identify and ask about locations.	_____	_____
2. Describe housing.	_____	_____
3. Identify types of transportation.	_____	_____
4. Express transportation preferences.	_____	_____
5. Give and follow directions.	_____	_____

My favorite lesson in this unit is _____.

Team Project

Describe your community.

1. Form a team with four or five students. In your team, you need:

POSITION	JOB	STUDENT NAME
Student 1: Team Leader	See that everyone speaks English. See that everyone participates.	
Student 2: Writer	Write directions.	
Student 3: Artist	Make a map.	
Student 4/5: Spokesperson	Prepare a presentation.	

2. Make a list of types of transportation in your community.

3. Make a map of your community with the school in the middle. Write the names of stores and other places near your school.

4. Write directions from your school to three places in your community.

5. Present your project to the class.

UNIT 6

Healthy Living

GOALS

➤ Identify body parts
➤ Describe symptoms and illnesses

➤ Identify medications
➤ Describe healthy habits
➤ Identify actions in a waiting room

LESSON 1

I need a checkup.

GOAL ➤ Identify body parts

Vocabulary   Grammar
Life Skills
Academic   Pronunciation

A Look at the picture.

Where is Guillermo?
Who is he talking to?

B Listen and write.

CD 2
TR 16

My name is Guillermo. _____ live in Chicago. I _____ 61 years old. I _____ the doctor once a year for a checkup. I'm very healthy.

GOAL ➤ Identify body parts

C Read the new words.

head	back	hand	foot
neck	arm	leg	nose

D Write the new words in the picture.

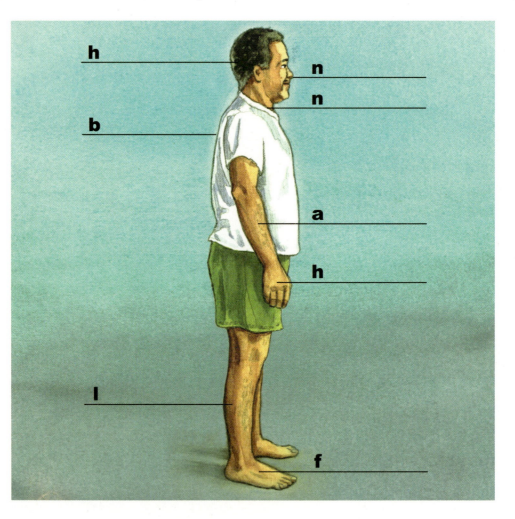

h _____
n _____
n _____
b _____
a _____
h _____
l _____
f _____

E Talk to a partner.

A: Where's the nose?
B: It's here. (points to own nose)

GOAL ➤ **Identify body parts**

F **Read.**

Imperatives		
	Subject	**Verb**
Please	~~you~~	read open let me (look) sit down stand up

Please read the chart.

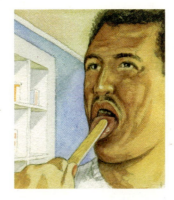

Please open your
mouth and say "Ah."

Let me look
in your ear.

CD 2
TR 17

G **Listen and practice the conversation.**

Doctor: Please sit down.
Guillermo: OK.
Doctor: Please open your mouth and say, "Ah."
Guillermo: Ah.

H **Practice the conversation with a partner. Use new sentences.**

I **What body parts are most important to you? Take a class poll.**

1. _____   3. _____

2. _____   4. _____

I'm sick!

GOAL ➤ Describe symptoms and illnesses

Vocabulary Grammar
Life Skills
Academic Pronunciation

A Listen and repeat.

CD 2
TR 18

headache

backache

stomachache

cold and runny nose

cough and sore throat

fever

B Listen and point.

CD 2
TR 19-24

C Read the conversation. Practice it with a partner. Use new words.

Maritza: How are you?
Shan: I'm sick!
Maritza: What's the matter?
Shan: I have <u>a headache</u>.

D   Read the charts.

Simple Present (Regular)		
Subject	**Verb**	**Example sentence**
I, you, we, they	see	I **see** the doctor once a year.
	visit	We **visit** the doctor once a year.
he, she, it	sees	He **sees** the doctor once a week.
	visits	She **visits** the doctor once a week.

Simple Present (Irregular)		
Subject	**Be**	**Example sentence**
I	am	I **am** sick.
you, we, they	are	We **are** sick.
he, she, it	is	He **is** sick.

Simple Present (Irregular)		
Subject	**Have**	**Example sentence**
I, you, we, they	have	I **have** a headache.
he, she, it	has	She **has** a runny nose.

E   Write.

1. He _____ has _____ (have) a headache.

2. She _____ (be) very sick.

3. We _____ (see) the doctor.

4. I _____ (be) sick.

5. You _____ (have) a cold.

6. Oscar _____ (have) a stomachache.

7. Maritza _____ (visit) the doctor once a year.

8. You _____ (be) sick.

9. We _____ (be) tired.

10. I _____ (like) my doctor.

11. The student _____ (have) a fever.

12. He _____ (be) a good doctor.

GOAL ➤ **Describe symptoms and illnesses**

 F Listen and bubble in the correct answer.

CD 2
TR 25-28

1. Maritza has
   ○ a cold.
   ○ a headache.
   ○ a fever.

2. Shan has
   ○ a backache.
   ○ a fever.
   ○ a cold.

3. John has
   ○ a runny nose.
   ○ a fever.
   ○ a headache.

4. Anakiya has
   ○ a fever.
   ○ a runny nose.
   ○ a backache.

G How many times a year are you sick? Write.

Headache	Stomachache	Backache	Fever	Cold

H Talk to four classmates. Then, fill in the chart.

A: John, how often do you have a headache?
B: I have a headache four times a year.

How often?	
once	a year
two times	a month
three times	a week
four times	a day

Name	Headache	Stomachache	Backache	Fever	Cold

LESSON  **3**

You need aspirin.

GOAL ▶ Identify medications

CD 2
TR 29

A Read, listen, and write the missing words.

February 18

Name	Time	Problem	Phone
Julio Rodriguez	3:30		(777) 555-1395
Huong Pham	4:00	fever	(777) 555-3311
Richard Price	4:30		(777) 555-2323
Mele Ikahihifo	5:00	sore throat and cough	(777) 555-5511
Fred Wharton	5:30		(777) 555-9764
Ayumi Tanaka	6:00	backache	(777) 555-8765

B Write the problems.

fever
_____

_____

_____

Have	
I, you, we, they	*have*
he, she	*has*

_____

_____

_____

C Write sentences.

1. Julio has a headache. _____

2. Richard has _____.

3. Ayumi _____.

GOAL ➤ Identify medications

D Look at the medicine bottles.

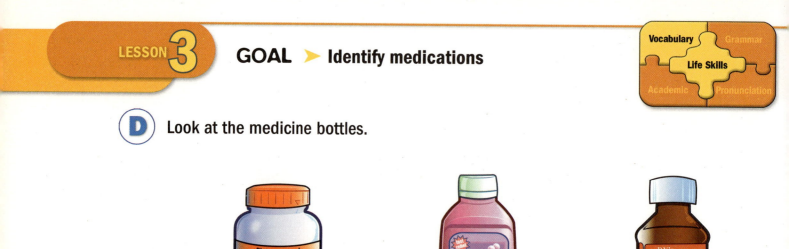

Phd. Approved
Extra Strength
ASPIRIN

fast relief
Antacid

RX's
Cough
Syrup
Cherry Flavor

Caution: Do not take more than four times a day.

E Write other types of medicine you take.

_____   _____   _____

F In a group, write a medicine for each illness.

Illness	Medicine
headache	
fever	
stomachache	
sore throat and cough	
cold	

GOAL ➤ Identify medications

G Read.

Simple Present		
I, you, we, they	need	aspirin
he, she, it	needs	antacid

H Write sentences. Use *need*.

1. Julio has a headache. He needs aspirin. _____
2. Huong has a fever. He _____.
3. Richard has a stomachache. He _____.
4. Mele has a sore throat and cough. She _____.
5. Fred has a cold. He _____.
6. Ayumi and Sue have backaches. They _____.
7. Tami and I have stomachaches. We _____.
8. Shiuli and Sang have sore throats. They _____.
9. You have a cold. You _____.
10. You have a headache. You _____.
11. We have sore throats. We _____.
12. We have fevers. We _____.

I What types of medicine do you have at home? Write.

_____ _____ _____ _____

J **Active Task.** Go to a pharmacy. Look for more types of medicine. Make a list and share it with the class.

Exercise every day!

GOAL ➤ Describe healthy habits

 A Read and listen.

CD 2
TR 30

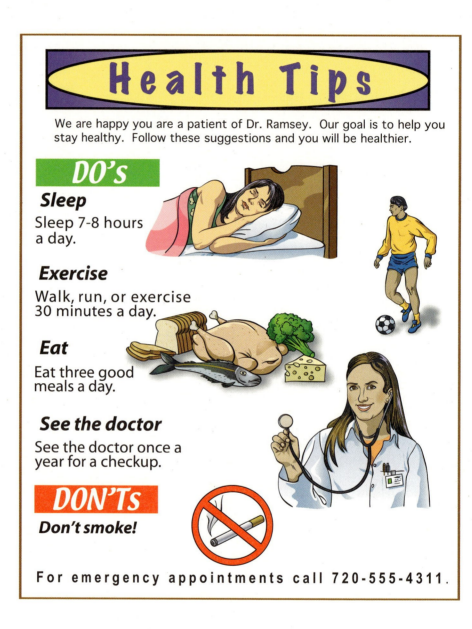

Health Tips

We are happy you are a patient of Dr. Ramsey. Our goal is to help you stay healthy. Follow these suggestions and you will be healthier.

DO's

Sleep
Sleep 7-8 hours a day.

Exercise
Walk, run, or exercise 30 minutes a day.

Eat
Eat three good meals a day.

See the doctor
See the doctor once a year for a checkup.

DON'Ts

Don't smoke!

For emergency appointments call 720-555-4311.

B Practice with a partner.

Dr. Ramsey: How many hours do you sleep a day?
Hasna: I sleep five hours a day.
Dr. Ramsey: That is not healthy. You need to sleep seven to eight hours.

GOAL ➤ Describe healthy habits

C Listen and read Huong's story. Why is Huong healthy?

CD 2
TR 31

    I'm healthy. I exercise one hour every day. I eat breakfast, lunch, and dinner. I don't eat a lot of candy. I don't smoke. I sleep seven hours every night.

D What does Huong do? Fill in the chart.

What does Huong do?	What doesn't Huong do?
exercise	

E Read the charts.

Simple Present		
Subject	**Verb**	**Example sentence**
I, you, we, they	eat	I **eat** three meals a day.
he, she, it	sleep**s**	She **sleeps** seven hours a night.

Negative Simple Present			
Subject	**Verb**		**Example sentence**
I, you, we, they	**don't**	eat	We **don't eat** three meals a day.
he, she, it	**doesn't**	sleep~~s~~	He **doesn't sleep** seven hours a day.

F Write about Huong.

1. Huong _____exercises_____ (exercise) one hour every day.

2. Huong _____ (sleep) seven hours every night.

3. Huong _____ (eat) breakfast, lunch, and dinner.

4. Huong _____ (smoke).

5. Huong _____ (eat) a lot of candy.

GOAL ➤ Describe healthy habits

G Read.

Name: Julia
Sleep: 8 hours
Meals: breakfast,
         lunch, dinner
Exercise: 30 minutes
            a day
Checkup: 1 time a year
Smoke: no

Name: Hasna
Sleep: 5 hours
Meals: lunch, dinner
Exercise: 0 minutes
            a day
Checkup: 1 time a year
Smoke: no

Name: Dalmar
Sleep: 8 hours
Meals: breakfast,
         lunch, dinner
Exercise: 20 minutes
            a day
Checkup: 0 times a year
Smoke: yes

H Write.

1. Julia and Hasna ____don't smoke____ (smoke).

2. Hasna _____ (eat) breakfast.

3. Dalmar and Julia _____ (sleep) eight hours every day.

4. Hasna _____ (exercise).

5. Julia and Hasna _____ (see) the doctor for a checkup.

6. Dalmar _____ (see) the doctor for a checkup.

I Write.

Your name: _____   **Exercise:** _____

Sleep: _____   **Checkup:** _____

Meals: _____   **Smoke:** _____

I have an appointment.

GOAL ➤ Identify actions in a waiting room

A Use the words in the box to talk about the picture.

talk   wait   read   answer   sleep

B Listen to the conversation. What words do you hear first? Write 1–5.

CD 2
TR 32

___ talk (are talking)

_1_ wait (are waiting)

___ read (is reading)

___ answer (am answering)

___ sleep (is sleeping)

C Read the chart.

Present Continuous (right now)			
Subject	**Be verb**	**Base + ing**	**Example sentence**
I	am	talking	I **am talking**.
he, she, it	is	sleeping	He **is sleeping**.
we, you, they	are	waiting	They **are waiting**.

Pronunciation

/g/
ing

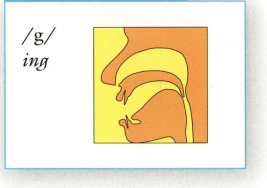

D Look at the picture on page 113. Write.

1. The receptionist <u>is</u> <u>answering</u> (answer) the phone now.

2. The man in the white shirt ____ _____ (sleep) in the chair now.

3. The people ____ _____ (wait) for the doctor now.

4. The women ____ _____ (talk) about their children now.

5. Antonio ____ _____ (read) a magazine now.

E Talk to a partner.

What is the receptionist doing now?
What is the man in the white shirt doing now?
What are the people doing now?
What are the women doing now?
What is Antonio doing now?

F Look at the picture.

RECEPTIONIST

G Talk about the picture with a partner.

H Imagine you are in a waiting room. Write sentences.

1. I'm _____

2. _____

3. _____

4. _____

Review

A Write the body parts. (Lesson 1)

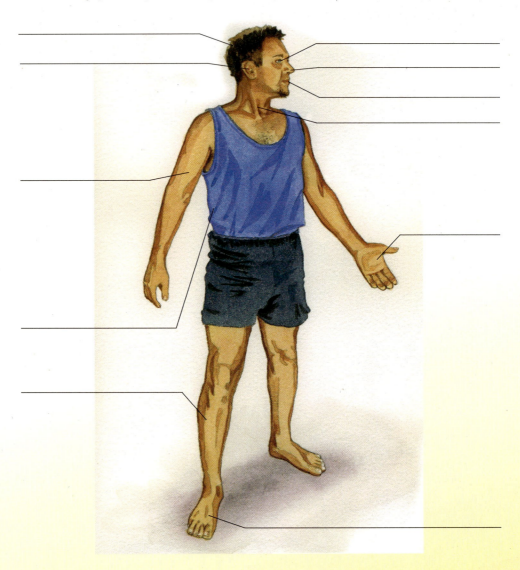

B Write the symptom or illness. (Lesson 2)

stomach _____stomachache_____

head _____

back _____

throat _____

nose _____

Complete the sentences with the present continuous. (Lesson 5)

1. The receptionist _____ _____ (talk) on the phone.

2. The patient is _____ _____ (sleep).

3. The people _____ _____ (wait) for the doctor.

4. The women _____ _____ (ask) about their children.

5. Hector _____ _____ (read) a magazine.

  Write. (Lesson 3)

1. Richard has a headache. What does he need?

   Medicine: _____

2. Orlando has a stomachache. What does he need?

   Medicine: _____

3. Hue has a fever. What does she need?

   Medicine: _____

4. Chan has a sore throat. What does he need?

   Medicine: _____

  Read and write in the chart. (Lesson 4)

Jeremiah is not very healthy. He smokes ten cigarettes a day. He doesn't exercise. He eats one meal a day. He doesn't sleep eight hours a night. He doesn't drink water. He sees the doctor once a year.

What does Jeremiah do?	What doesn't Jeremiah do?

Review

F Complete the sentences with the simple present. (Lessons 2 and 4)

1. She _____ (have) a headache.

2. They _____ (need) medicine.

3. We _____ (be) sick.

4. I _____ (be) healthy.

5. You _____ (exercise) every day.

6. Mario and Maria _____ (visit) the doctor.

7. He _____ (sleep) eight hours a day.

8. Alfonso _____ (smoke) cigarettes.

G Complete the sentences with the negative simple present. (Lesson 4)

1. He _____ (smoke) every day.

2. They _____ (eat) breakfast.

3. We _____ (need) medicine.

4. They _____ (exercise).

5. Nga _____ (have) a headache.

6. She _____ (visit) the doctor.

7. I _____ (want) lunch.

8. You _____ (exercise).

My Dictionary

Make flash cards to improve your vocabulary.

1. Choose four new words from this unit.
2. Write each word on an index card or on a piece of paper.
3. On the back of the index card or on a paper, draw a picture, find and write a sentence from the book with the word, and write the page number.
4. Study the words.

Julio has a headache.

page 109

Learner Log

Write the page number(s).

	Page Number	I can do it. ✓
1. Identify body parts.	_____	_____
2. Describe symptoms and illnesses.	_____	_____
3. Identify medications.	_____	_____
4. Describe healthy habits.	_____	_____
5. Identify actions in a waiting room.	_____	_____

My favorite lesson in this unit is _____.

Team Project

Write conversations and create an appointment book page.

February 18			
Name	Time	Problem	Phone
Julio Rodriguez	3:30		(777) 555-1395
Huong Pham	4:00	fever	(777) 555-3311
Richard Price	4:30		(777) 555-2323
Mele Ikahihifo	5:00	sore throat and cough	(777) 555-5511
Fred Wharton	5:30		(777) 555-9764
Ayumi Tanaka	6:00	backache	(777) 555-8765

1. Form a team with four or five students.
   In your team, you need:

POSITION	JOB	STUDENT NAME
Student 1: Team Leader	See that everyone speaks English. See that everyone participates.	
Student 2: Writer	Write conversations to act out.	
Student 3: Artist	Make an appointment book page.	
Students 4/5: Spokespeople	Prepare a presentation.	

2. Prepare your roles.

   Who is the doctor? _____

   Who is Patient 1? _____

   Who is Patient 2? _____

   Who is the receptionist? _____

3. Make an appointment book page.

   What is Patient 1's name?
   When is the appointment?
   What is the problem?
   Write a conversation between the receptionist and Patient 1.
   Write a conversation between the doctor and Patient 1.

4. Write conversations for Patient 2.

5. Present your conversations and appointment book page to the class.

Work

GOALS

➤ Identify occupations
➤ Give information about work
➤ Identify job duties

➤ Read evaluations
➤ Read signs and follow directions

LESSON **1**

Do you work?

GOAL ➤ Identify occupations

A Talk about the picture.

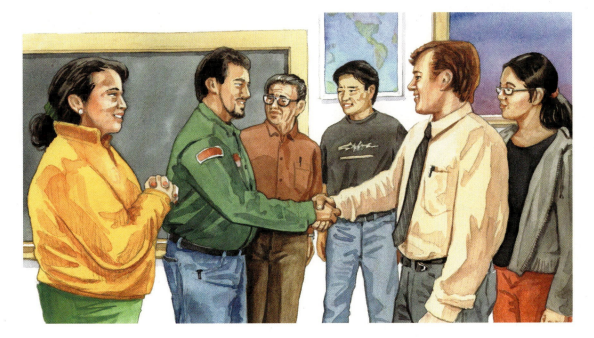

B Listen and read.

CD 2
TR 33

My name is Emilio. I live in Dallas, Texas. I have a new job. I'm a cashier at Ultra Supermarket on Broadway! This is a picture of my English class.

C Write. What does Emilio do?

He's a student, and he's also a _____.

Vocabulary   Grammar
Life Skills
Academic   Pronunciation

CD 2
TR 34

D   Listen and repeat the words. What do these people do?

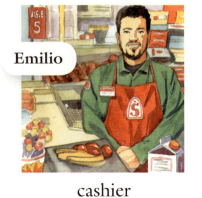

Emilio

Hue

Chan

cashier   doctor   bus driver

Carolina

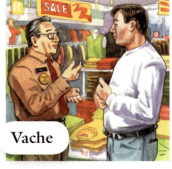

Vache

Pete

student   salesperson   teacher

E   Practice the conversation with a partner. Use the words in Exercise D.

A: What does <u>Emilio</u> do?
B: He's a <u>cashier</u>.

F   Write sentences about the people in Exercise D.

1. <u>Emilio is a cashier.</u>

2. <u>Hue</u>

3. _____

4. _____

5. _____

6. _____

GOAL ➤ Identify occupations

Vocabulary   Grammar
Life Skills
Academic   Pronunciation

| cook | custodian | mail carrier | manager | nurse |

 G   Who works here? Write the jobs in the chart.

School	Restaurant	Clothing store	Community	Doctor's office
teacher	cashier	salesperson	bus driver	doctor

 H   Practice the conversation.
Make new conversations.

A: Where does <u>a teacher</u> work?
B: He works in <u>a school</u>.

Simple Present	
I work.	I don't work.
He works.	He doesn't work.
She works.	She doesn't work.

I   Read the conversation.

A: Do you work?
B: Yes, I work. I'm a cashier. How about you? Do you work?
A: No, I don't work. I'm a student.

 J   Practice the conversation with four classmates.

Name	Occupation

K   **Active Task.** What do your friends and family do? Make a list.

When do you go to work?

GOAL ➤ **Give information about work**

 A Listen.

CD 2
TR 35

1.

Name: Isabel
Title: receptionist
Company: Johnson Company
Supervisor: Martin
Hours: 9 A.M.–6 P.M.
Break: 12 P.M.–1 P.M.
Days: Monday–Friday

2.

Name: Colleen
Title: manager
Company: Freedman's Foods
Supervisor: Amelia
Hours: 2 P.M.–10 P.M.
Break: 6 P.M.–7 P.M.
Days: Wednesday–Sunday

3.

Name: Fred
Title: custodian
Company: America Bank
Supervisor: Mary
Hours: 10 P.M.–7 A.M.
Break: 1 A.M.–2 A.M.
Days: Sunday–Friday

B Listen and write the names of the people from Exercise A.

CD 2
TR 36

1. _____   2. _____   3. _____

GOAL ➤ **Give information about work**

C Read.

Information Questions	
Question word	**Type of answer**
What	information (receptionist)
Where	a place (Johnson Company)
When	a time or day (9–6) (Monday–Friday)
Who	a person (Martin)

D Match the questions and answers about Colleen.

1. What do you do?
2. Where do you work?
3. Who is your supervisor?
4. When do you work?
5. When is your break?

a. I work at Freedman's Foods.
b. It's from 6:00 P.M.–7:00 P.M.
c. I work Wednesday through Sunday.
d. I'm a manager.
e. Amelia.

E With a partner, answer the questions. Take turns being Fred.

1. What do you do, Fred?
2. Where do you work?
3. Who is your supervisor?
4. When do you work?
5. When is your break?

F Ask and answer questions about Isabel.

EXAMPLE: *A: What* does Isabel do?
 B: She's a receptionist.

GOAL ➤ Give information about work

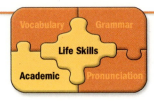

G Read.

My name is Ben. I'm a nurse. I work at a hospital from 7:00 A.M. to 7:00 P.M. I work Monday through Thursday. I help the doctors and talk to patients. My supervisor is Mrs. O'Malley.

H Answer the questions.

1. What does Ben do? He's a _____.

2. When does he start work? He starts work at _____.

3. Where does he work? He works at _____.

4. Who is Ben's supervisor? She is _____.

 I Listen. Fill in the chart about Tan, Maria, and Alfredo.

CD 2
TR 37-39

	What	When	Where
Tan	custodian		
Maria			
Alfredo			

J Answer the questions.

1. What do you do? _____

2. Where do you work or go to school? _____

3. Who is your supervisor or teacher? _____

4. When do you work or go to school? _____

What do you do?

GOAL ▶ **Identify job duties**

A Listen and point.

CD 2
TR 40

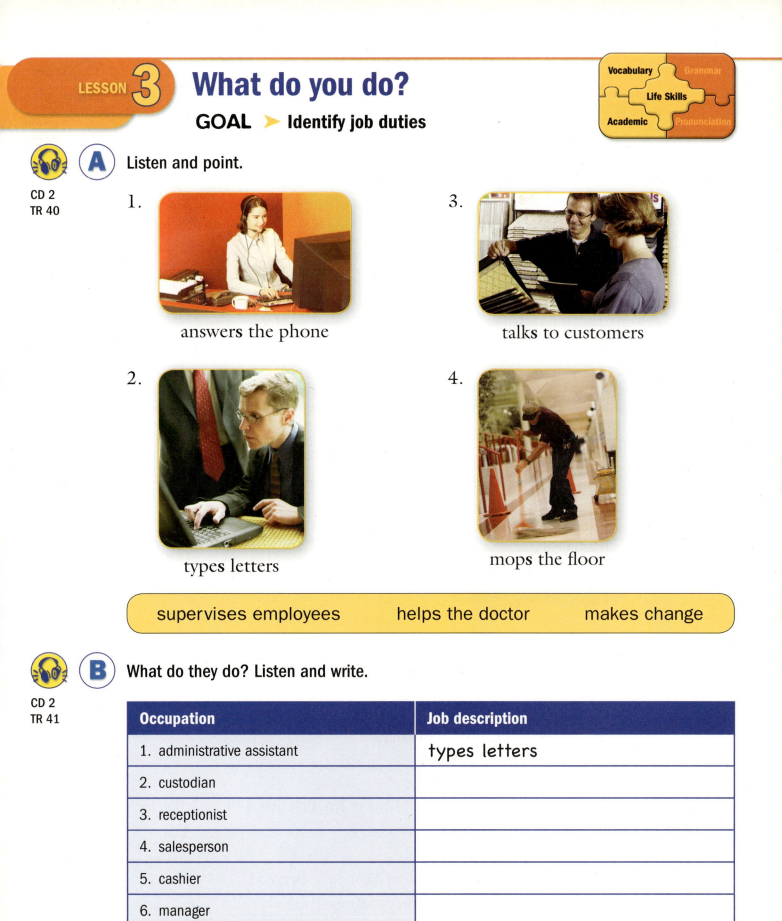

1.

answers the phone

3.

talks to customers

2.

types letters

4.

mops the floor

| supervises employees | helps the doctor | makes change |

B What do they do? Listen and write.

CD 2
TR 41

Occupation	Job description
1. administrative assistant	types letters
2. custodian	
3. receptionist	
4. salesperson	
5. cashier	
6. manager	
7. nurse	

LESSON 3 **GOAL** ➤ Identify job duties

C Read.

A receptionist files papers.

Sometimes workers take breaks.

	mops	answers phones	talks to customers	types letters	takes breaks	files papers
salesperson		X	X		X	
administrative assistant		X		X	X	X
receptionist		X	X		X	X
custodian	X				X	

Pronunciation

Yes/No **Questions**

➤ Does he file?
➤ Does she type?
➤ Does he talk to customers?

D Answer the questions. Check (✓) *Yes* or *No*. Practice with a partner.

		Yes	No
1.	Does a salesperson file?	_____	✓
2.	Does an administrative assistant take breaks?	_____	_____
3.	Does a custodian talk to customers?	_____	_____
4.	Does a receptionist talk to customers?	_____	_____
5.	Does a salesperson mop the floors?	_____	_____

GOAL ➤ Identify job duties

E Read.

Can			
Subject	**Can**	**Verb (base)**	**Example sentence**
I, you, he, she, it, we, they	can	type	I can type.
		mop	He can mop floors.

Can't			
Subject	**Can't**	**Verb (base)**	**Example sentence**
I, you, he, she, it, we, they	can't	type	I can't type.
		mop	He can't mop floors.

F Complete the sentences with *can* + the verb.

1. He _____can file_____ (file) papers.

2. They _____ (type) letters.

3. I _____ (mop) the floor.

4. You _____ (answer) phones.

G Complete the sentences with *can't* + the verb.

1. We _____can't take_____ (take) breaks.

2. They _____ (type).

3. I _____ (talk) to customers.

4. She _____ (file).

H Write what you *can* and *can't* do. Use words from this lesson.

1. I can _____.   1. I can't _____.

2. _____.   2. _____.

LESSON **4** **You're doing great!**

GOAL ➤ Read evaluations

A Read.

Work Evaluation

Name: _Emilio Sanchez_

Helps customers	(Yes)	No
Comes to work on time	(Yes)	No
Speaks English well	(Yes)	No
Follows directions well	(Yes)	No

Manager Signature: _Calvin Carter_

B What does a good student do? Circle.

files	practices English
(listens)	takes lunch breaks
cleans the office	follows directions
types letters	writes in class
does homework	reads in class
talks to customers	speaks in class
comes to school on time	answers phones

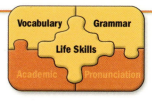

C Read.

Simple Present: *Be*		
Subject	*Be*	Example sentence
I	am	I **am** friendly.
he, she, it	is	She **is** friendly.
we, you, they	are	They **are** friendly.

Simple Present: *Be* (negative)		
Subject	*Be* (Negative)	Example sentence
I	am not	I **am not** friendly.
he, she, it	is not	She **is not** friendly.
we, you, they	are not	They **are not** friendly.

| friendly   helpful   careful   cheerful |

D Write the *be* verb.

1. Emilio _____ friendly with the customers.

2. Carolina _____ not cheerful.

3. We _____ helpful.

4. They _____ not careful.

E Listen and circle.

CD 2
TR 42

Work Evaluation

Name: *Chan Chin*

Is careful	Yes	No
Is friendly	Yes	No
Is helpful	Yes	No
Is cheerful	Yes	No

Manager Signature: *Jim Brown*

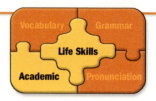

 F Read.

Vache Deluse is a salesperson. He works every day, Monday through Friday. He always helps customers and he is always friendly. Sometimes he is not careful with clothing, and sometimes he doesn't come to work on time.

 G Complete the evaluation.

Work Evaluation

Name: _Vache Deluse_		
Helps customers	Yes	No
Comes to work on time	Yes	No
Is friendly	Yes	No
Is careful	Yes	No
Manager Signature: _Calvin Carter_		

H Complete an evaluation for yourself at school.

My Evaluation

I come to school on time.	Yes	No
I follow directions.	Yes	No
I do my homework.	Yes	No
I am cheerful and friendly.	Yes	No

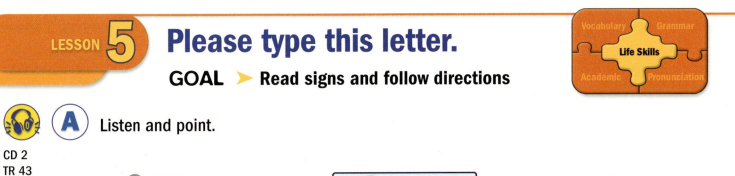

LESSON **5** **Please type this letter.**

GOAL ➤ **Read signs and follow directions**

A Listen and point.

CD 2
TR 43

1. Don't smoke.

2. Wash your hands.

3. File the papers.

For: *Fred*   ☐Urgent
Phone Call
Message: *Please answer the phones.*

4. Fred, please answer the phones.

Fred,
Please type these letters.

5. Fred, please type these letters.

6. Don't eat in the office.

B Read the signs and notes. Circle *Yes* or *No*.

1. Smoke.	Yes	(No)
2. Wash hands.	Yes	No
3. File.	Yes	No
4. Answer the phones.	Yes	No
5. Type letters.	Yes	No
6. Eat.	Yes	No

GOAL ➤ **Read signs and follow directions**

C Read.

Affirmative Commands			
	Verb		**Example sentence**
~~You~~	wash	your hands	Wash your hands.
	answer	the phones	Answer the phones.
	type	letters	Type the letters.

Negative Commands				
	Verb			**Example sentence**
~~You~~	don't	wash	your hands	Don't wash your hands.
		answer	the phones	Don't answer the phones.
		type	letters	Don't type the letters.

wash	answer	type	clean
file	eat	smoke	

D Complete the sentences.

1. Wash <u>your hands.</u> _____

2. Clean _____.

3. Answer _____.

4. Don't _____.

E Read and practice the conversations. Use the commands in Exercise C.

Manager: How are you, Isabel?
Isabel: I'm fine, thank you.
Manager: Please, <u>clean your desk today</u>.
Isabel: Yes, of course.

Manager: How are you, Isabel?
Isabel: I'm fine, thank you.
Manager: Please, <u>don't eat in the office</u>.
Isabel: No, of course not.

GOAL ➤ **Read signs and follow directions**

F Read.

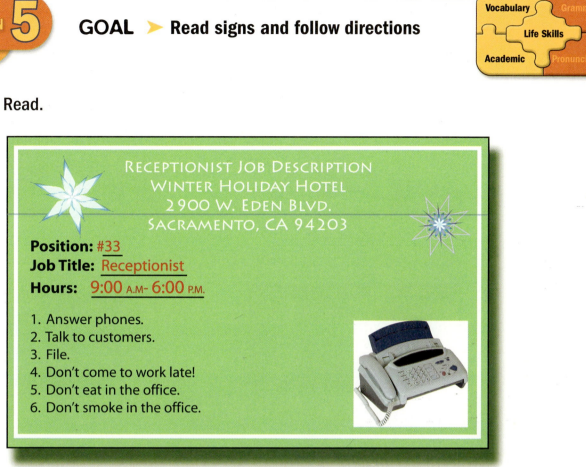

RECEPTIONIST JOB DESCRIPTION
WINTER HOLIDAY HOTEL
2900 W. EDEN BLVD.
SACRAMENTO, CA 94203

Position: #33
Job Title: Receptionist
Hours: 9:00 A.M– 6:00 P.M.

1. Answer phones.
2. Talk to customers.
3. File.
4. Don't come to work late!
5. Don't eat in the office.
6. Don't smoke in the office.

G Look at the job description in Exercise F. Write the commands.

Do's	Don'ts
Answer phones.	

H In groups, write classroom *do's* and *don'ts.*

Classroom Do's	Classroom Don'ts
Listen.	

Review

A Write the name of the job. (Lesson 1)

1.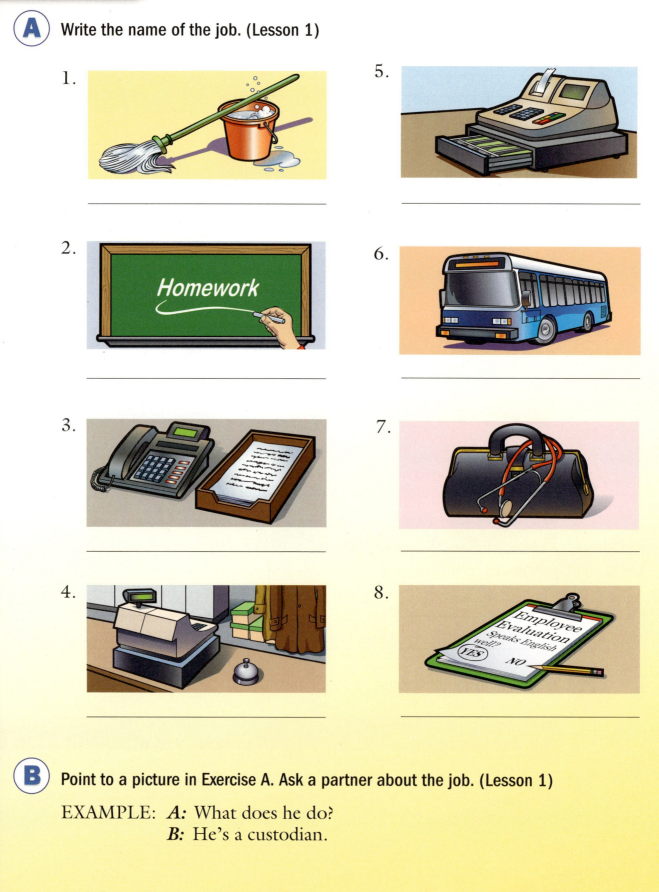

_____

2.

_____

3.

_____

4.

_____

5.

_____

6.

_____

7.

_____

8.

_____

B Point to a picture in Exercise A. Ask a partner about the job. (Lesson 1)

EXAMPLE: *A:* What does he do?
                   B: He's a custodian.

C Match the job with the duty. Draw a line. (Lessons 1 and 3)

1.

a. types letters

2.

b. makes change

3.

c. mops the floor

4.

d. talks to customers

D Write *when, where, what,* or *who.* (Lesson 2)

1. _____ does the store open? The store opens at 10:00 A.M.

2. _____ do you take a break? I take a break in the cafeteria.

3. _____ do you work? I work in Sacramento.

4. _____ is your manager? His name is Martin.

5. _____ does she do? She's a nurse.

E Identify the signs. (Lesson 5)

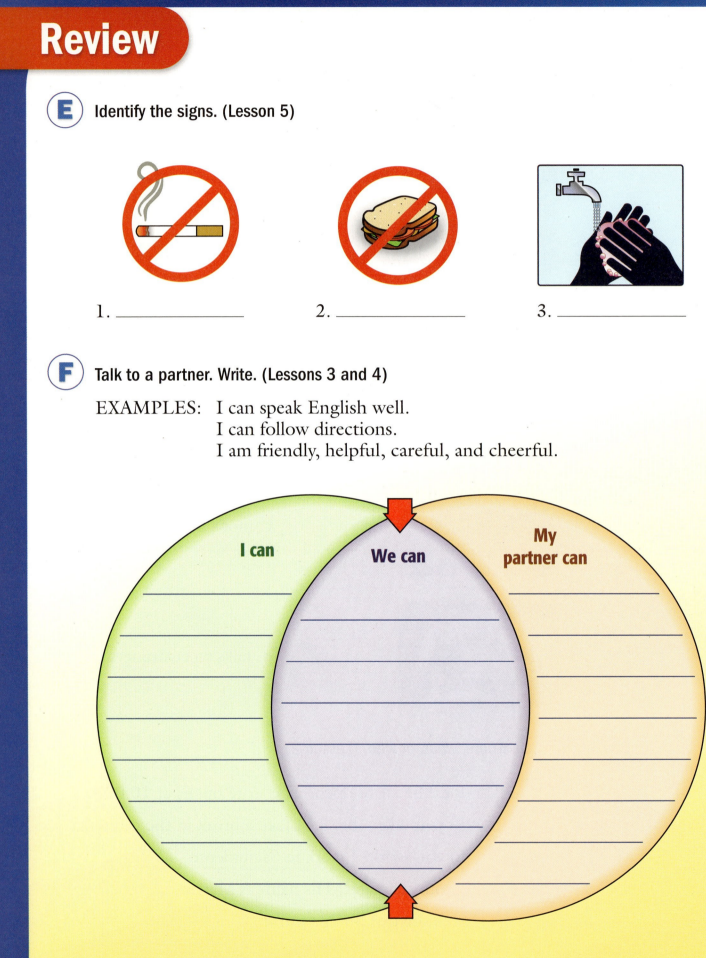

1. _____

2. _____

3. _____

F Talk to a partner. Write. (Lessons 3 and 4)

EXAMPLES: I can speak English well.
I can follow directions.
I am friendly, helpful, careful, and cheerful.

I can

We can

My partner can

My Dictionary

Make flash cards to improve your vocabulary.

1. Choose four new words from this unit.
2. Write each word on an index card or on a piece of paper.
3. On the back of the index card or paper, draw a picture, find and write a sentence from the book with the word, and write the page number.
4. Study the words.

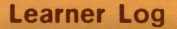

I'm a manager.

page 125

Learner Log

Write the page number(s).

	Page Number	I can do it. ✓
1. Identify occupations.	_____	_____
2. Ask questions with *when* and *where*.	_____	_____
3. Talk about job duties.	_____	_____
4. Use *can* and *can't*.	_____	_____
5. Discuss do's and don'ts.	_____	_____

My favorite page in this unit is _____.

Team Project

Start a company.

1. Form a team with four or five students. In your team, you need:

POSITION	JOB	STUDENT NAME
Student 1: Team Leader	See that everyone speaks English. See that everyone participates.	
Student 2: Writer	Write job descriptions.	
Student 3: Artist	Make a cover page with the name of your company and a logo.	
Students 4/5: Spokespeople	Prepare a presentation.	

2. What is the name of your company?
   What is your company logo? Make a cover page.

3. What are the occupations in the company?

4. Write three job descriptions for jobs in your company.

5. Present your company to the class.

Lifelong Learning and Review

GOALS

➤ **Organize study materials**
➤ **Make purchases**
➤ **Give and follow directions**
➤ **Make goals**
➤ **Develop a study schedule**

LESSON 1

Let's get organized!

GOAL ➤ **Organize study materials**

Vocabulary Grammar
Life Skills
Academic Pronunciation

CD 2
TR 44

A Listen and repeat.

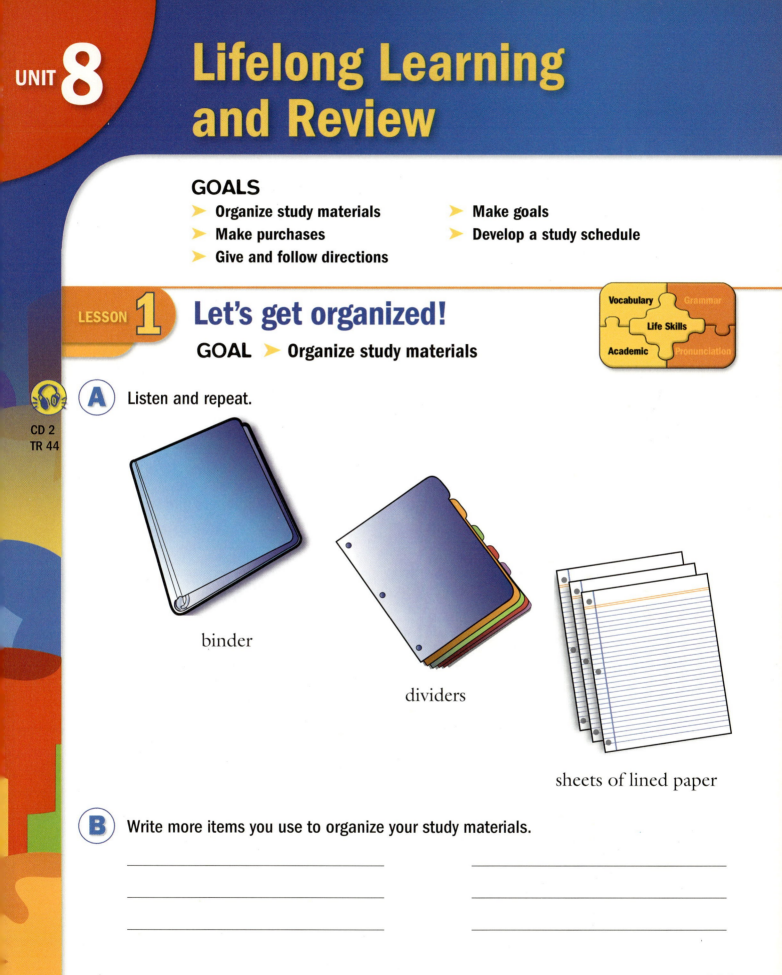

binder

dividers

sheets of lined paper

B Write more items you use to organize your study materials.

_____   _____

_____   _____

_____   _____

GOAL ➤ **Organize study materials**

 C Listen and bubble in.

CD 2
TR 45

1. What size binder do they need?
   ○ 1 inch
   ○ 1 ½ inches
   ○ 3 inches

2. How many dividers do they need?
   ○ 1 divider
   ○ 3 dividers
   ○ 5 dividers

3. How many sheets of lined paper do they need?
   ○ 50 sheets
   ○ 100 sheets
   ○ 200 sheets

D Look through Units 1–7 of your book. Write the page numbers and two words for each section in your binder.

Section	Reference pages	Example vocabulary
Personal Information	1–40	
Consumer Economics (FOOD/CLOTHING)		
Community Resources		
Health		
Occupational Knowledge		

GOAL ➤ Organize study materials

 Interview and write about your partner. Report to a group.

1. What's your name? _____

2. Where do you live? _____

3. What is your phone number? _____

4. What is your birth date? _____

5. Are you married? _____

6. Where are you from? _____

***Be* Verb**
I am . . .
My phone number is . . .

F Make the first page in your binder on a sheet of paper.

PERSONAL PROFILE

_____
SCHOOL

| PHOTO |

_____
TEACHER

NAME _____
     First   Middle   Last

ADDRESS _____

CITY _____ STATE _____ ZIP _____

COUNTRY _____

MARITAL STATUS *(Circle)*   Single   Married   Divorced

LESSON 2

I need paper.

GOAL ➤ Make purchases

Vocabulary · Grammar · Life Skills · Academic · Pronunciation

A Read the advertisements.

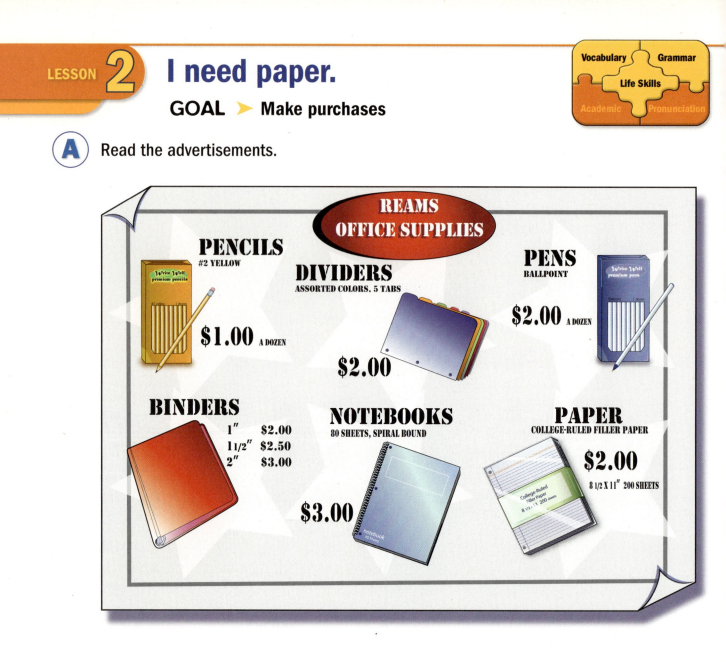

> How much **is** the paper?   How much **are** the notebooks?

B Listen to the conversation and practice.

CD 2
TR 46

Customer: Excuse me, how much are the dividers?
Salesperson: They are $2.00 for a set of five.
Customer: Thanks. I need one set, please.

GOAL ➤ Make purchases

C Listen and repeat.

CD 2
TR 47

I need …
> a box of pencils.
> a two-inch binder.
> a set of five colored dividers.
> a package of paper.
> a box of ballpoint pens.
> a notebook.

> a two-inch binder = a 2" binder

D What do you need? Write.

REAMS OFFICE SUPPLIES

Item	Quantity	Price
2" Binder	1	$3.00
		Total

Customer Copy

E Practice the conversation. Use information from Exercise A on page 144.

Salesperson: What do you need?
Customer: I need a <u>two-inch binder</u>.
Salesperson: They are over here.
Customer: How much are they?
Salesperson: They are <u>$3.00</u> each.

F **Active Task.** Go to a store in your community and buy office supplies.

GOAL ➤ **Make purchases**

G In a group, make a list of food you buy in the supermarket.

Food	Price

H In a group, make a list of clothing you buy in a clothing store.

Clothing	Price

I Look at Exercise E on page 145. Write and practice new conversations about food and clothing.

J Prepare a section in your binder for Consumer Economics.

Consumer Economics

Stand Out Basic Page Numbers _____

Important Vocabulary

Food:
apples
_____ _____ _____ _____
_____ _____ _____ _____

Clothing:
shoes
_____ _____ _____ _____
_____ _____ _____ _____

Sentences and Questions

What's for lunch?
I need a blue shirt.
_____ _____
_____ _____
_____ _____
_____ _____
_____ _____

Consumer Economics

Grammar
Prepositions of Location   Page Number: _____

Singular and Plural   Page Number: _____

Simple Present - *like*   Page Number: _____

Where's the office supply store?

GOAL ➤ Give and follow directions

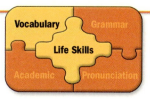

A Look at the picture.

CD 2
TR 48

B Listen to the conversation. Write.

Linda: Excuse me, where is Reams Office Supplies?
Officer: It's on First Street.
Linda: On First Street?
Officer: Yes, go straight on this street. Turn _____ on Main Street

and _____ on First. It's _____ the video store.
Linda: Thanks.

GOAL ➤ Give and follow directions

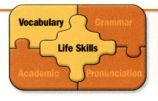

 C Read.

City Phone Directory

Nursing Schools	**Optometrists**

Ace Nursing Schools
8237 Beachnut Ave. ·············· 555-6732
Metropolitan Nursing
2467 Apple Lane ················· 555-3472

Dr. Michael's Eye Exams
1723 First St. ·················· 555-3310
Quick Check Glasses
3456 W. Circle Ave. ··············· 555-6776

Office Supply	**Painting Supplies**

Pencil Head Stationers
11 Broadway ················· 555-3411
Nottingham Paper
23400 Portland Ave ············· 555-0045
Reams Office Supply
1717 First St. ················· 555-2762

Bill's Painting Supply
5678 First St. ·················· 555-1301
Paint for Less
15 Broadway ·················· 555-3737
Picture Perfect

D Read the conversation.

Linda: Excuse me, where is <u>Reams Office Supplies</u>?
Officer: It's on <u>First Street</u>.
Linda: What's the address?
Officer: It's <u>1717 First Street</u>.
Linda: Thanks.

E Practice new conversations with the information in Exercise C.

GOAL ➤ Give and follow directions

 Draw a map from your school to an office supply store in your community.

Prepositions
It's *next to* the bank.
It's *between* the bank and the store.
It's *on* the corner.

G Write directions to the office supply store.

_____

_____

_____

_____

H Prepare a section in your binder for Community.

Community

Stand Out Basic Page Numbers

Important Vocabulary

left

Sentences and Questions

What's for lunch?
I need a blue shirt.

Community

Grammar
in/on   Page Number: _____

Simple Present   Page Number: _____

_____   Page Number: _____

LESSON 4 Sleep eight hours a day.

GOAL ➤ Make goals

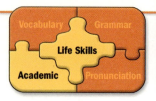

A Read Liang's goals.

> ### My Goals
>
> ☑ Sleep eight hours a day.
> ☐ Go to school every day.
> ☐ Exercise one hour a day.
> ☑ Eat three good meals a day.
> ☐ Study English at home one hour a day.
> ☑ Read the newspaper in English fifteen minutes a day.
> ☐ Watch TV fifteen minutes a day.

B Listen and check Carina's three goals.

CD 2
TR 49

☐ Sleep eight hours a day.

☐ Go to school every day.

☐ Exercise one hour a day.

☐ Eat three good meals a day.

☐ Study English at home one hour a day.

☐ Read the newspaper in English fifteen minutes a day.

☐ Watch TV fifteen minutes a day.

C Talk about Liang's and Carina's goals.

EXAMPLE: Liang's goal is to sleep eight hours a day.

GOAL ➤ **Make goals**

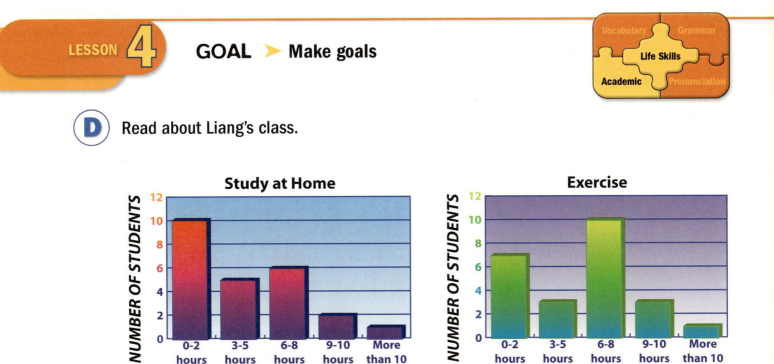

D Read about Liang's class.

Study at Home

Exercise

E Take a class poll. Make a bar graph.

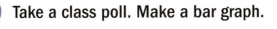

Study at Home

NUMBER OF STUDENTS

| 0-2 hours | 3-5 hours | 6-8 hours | 9-10 hours | More than 10 |

HOURS A WEEK

GOAL ➤ **Make goals**

 Interview a partner. Write his or her answers.

1. How many hours do you exercise every day? _____

2. How many hours do you sleep every day? _____

3. How many hours do you study every day? _____

4. How many meals do you eat every day? _____

5. How many days do you go to school a week? _____

G Write your goals.

_____

_____

_____

_____

_____

_____

 Prepare a section in your binder for Health.

Health	
Stand Out Basic Page Numbers	
_____	
Important Vocabulary	
____ ____ ____ ____	
____ ____ ____ ____	
____ ____ ____ ____	
____ ____ ____ ____	
Sentences and Questions	
_____	
_____	
_____	

Health
Grammar
Simple Present   Page Number: _____
Negative Simple Present   Page Number: _____
Present Continuous   Page Number: _____

When can I study?

GOAL ➤ Develop a study schedule

 **A** Listen and point.

CD 2
TR 50

Teacher and Student Duties

help students	study at home	come to class on time
study new words	prepare lessons	do homework

 Write.

Student duties	Teacher duties
	help students

C Add more duties to the list in Exercise B.

GOAL ➤ **Develop a study schedule**

D Read and talk about the schedule. When does Liang work?

LIANG'S SCHEDULE

	Sunday	Monday	Tuesday	Wednesday	Thursday	Friday	Saturday
6:00 A.M.	Breakfast	Breakfast	Breakfast	Breakfast	Breakfast	Breakfast	Breakfast
9:00 A.M.		School	School	School	School	Study	Study
11:00 A.M.	Lunch	Lunch	Lunch	Lunch	Lunch	Lunch	Lunch
1:00 P.M.		Study	Study	Study	Study	Study	Study
3:00 P.M.							
5:00 P.M.		Work	Work	Work	Work	Work	
7:00 P.M.	Dinner	Dinner	Dinner	Dinner	Dinner	Dinner	Dinner
9:00 P.M.							

E Answer the questions.

1. When do you study at school?

   _____

2. When do you study at home?

   _____

3. When do you work? _____

4. When do you eat breakfast, lunch,

   and dinner? _____

Simple Present

I **study** one hour.

You **study** one hour.

We **study** one hour.

They **study** one hour.

He **studies** one hour.

She **studies** one hour.

F Complete your schedule.

MY SCHEDULE

	Sunday	Monday	Tuesday	Wednesday	Thursday	Friday	Saturday

GOAL ➤ Develop a study schedule

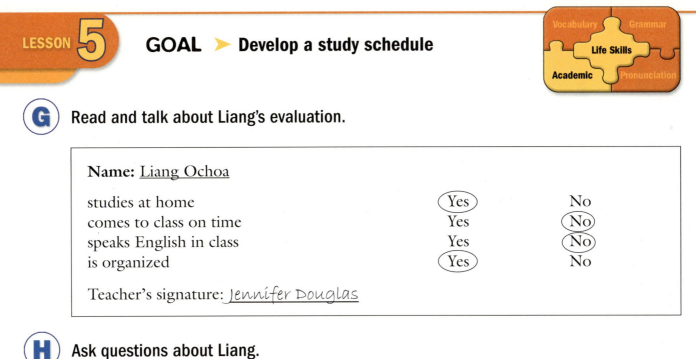

G Read and talk about Liang's evaluation.

Name: Liang Ochoa

studies at home	(Yes)	No
comes to class on time	Yes	(No)
speaks English in class	Yes	(No)
is organized	(Yes)	No

Teacher's signature: *Jennifer Douglas*

H Ask questions about Liang.

EXAMPLE: Does Liang study at home?

I Complete an evaluation about yourself. Ask your teacher to sign it.

Name: _____

studies at home	Yes	No
comes to class on time	Yes	No
speaks English in class	Yes	No
is organized	Yes	No

Teacher's signature: _____

J Prepare a section in your binder for Occupational Knowledge.

Occupational (Work) Knowledge

Stand Out Basic Page Numbers _____

Important Vocabulary

_____ _____ _____ _____

_____ _____ _____ _____

Sentences and Questions

_____ _____

Occupational (Work) Knowledge

Grammar
when/where   Page Number: _____

can/can't   Page Number: _____

Affirmative and negative instructions   Page Number: _____

Review

A Match. Draw a line.

1. January, _____, March
2. This person answers phones in an office.
3. It is at the end of your arm.
4. your home
5. milk, cheese, butter
6. not sunny
7. medicine for a headache
8. a place for money
9. food for a sandwich
10. ten cents
11. This person can work in a hospital.
12. May, _____, July
13. clothing for winter
14. a place to buy food
15. You wear them on your feet.
16. You _____ a bicycle.

a. dairy
b. address
c. aspirin
d. bank
e. bread
f. dime
g. doctor
h. February
i. hand
j. June
k. cloudy
l. receptionist
m. ride
n. shoes
o. supermarket
p. sweater

B Practice with a partner.

A: It is at the end of your arm.
B: hand

C Find the page number for the words. (You can look at the Vocabulary List on page 161.)

Word(s)	Page number	Word(s)	Page number
divorced		broccoli	
application		cash register	
foggy		healthy	
sit		mop	

Find the page number from the Vocabulary List on page 161 and write the sentence.

Phrase: marital status

Page number: __7__

Sentence: What's your marital status? _____

Phrase: extra large

Page number: ____

Sentence: _____

Phrase: go straight

Page number: ____

Sentence: _____

Word: checkup

Page number: ____

Sentence: _____

E **Find two new words from the Vocabulary List on page 161.**

Word: _____

Page number: ____

Sentence: _____

Word: _____

Page number: ____

Sentence: _____

Review

 F Use the Grammar Reference on pages 163–165 and fill in the blanks.

1. a. I _____ married.

   b. We _____ students.

   c. You _____ hungry.

   d. They _____ thirsty.

   e. She _____ single.

2. a. I _____ milk.

   b. We _____ a bowl of soup.

   c. You _____ vegetables.

   d. They _____ tacos.

   e. She _____ a sandwich.

3. a. _____ your hands.

   b. _____ the phones.

   c. _____ letters.

4. a. I can _____.

   b. They can _____.

   c. We can't _____.

   d. She can't _____.

G Write the plural forms.

Singular	Plural
pear	
cookie	
banana	
egg	
tomato	

My Dictionary

Make flash cards to improve your vocabulary.

1. Choose four new words from this unit.
2. Write each word on an index card or on a piece of paper.
3. On the back of the index card or paper, draw a picture, find and write a sentence from the book with the word, and write the page number.
4. Study the words.

I need a two-inch binder.

page 145

Learner Log

Write the page number(s).

	Page Number	I can do it. ✓
1. Personal information	_____	_____
2. How much is the binder?	_____	_____
3. Where is the store?	_____	_____
4. Goals	_____	_____
5. Schedules	_____	_____

My favorite page in this unit is _____.

Team Project

Create a study guide.

1. Form a team with four or five students. In your team, you need:

POSITION	JOB	STUDENT NAME
Student 1: Team Leader	See that everyone speaks English. See that everyone participates.	
Student 2: Writer	Organize and add sections to the study guide.	
Student 3: Artist	Decorate the study guide.	
Students 4/5: Spokespeople	Prepare a presentation.	

2. Complete your binder from this unit. Share the information from your binder with your group.

3. Use your binders to make a team binder. This will be a study guide for new students.

4. Decorate the study guide.

5. Present your study guide to the class.

Stand Out Basic Vocabulary List

Pre-Unit
Greetings
bye P1
goodbye P1
hello P1
hi P1
Study verbs
bubble in P9
circle P5
listen P17
point P4
practice P8
read P7
repeat P8
write P7

Unit 1
Calendar
date 14
day 14
month 13
week 13
year 13
Days
Sunday 13
Monday 13
Tuesday 13
Wednesday 13
Thursday 13
Friday 13
Saturday 13
Months
January 13
February 13
March 13
April 13
May 13
June 13
July 13
August 13
September 13
October 13
November 13
December 13
Marital status
divorced 7
married 7
single 7
Personal information
address 10
application 13
birth date 14
birthplace 5
city 10
name 1

state 10
zip code 10

Unit 2
from 4
live 6
phone number 28
schedule 30
time 31
Weather
cloudy 33
cold 33
foggy 33
hot 33
rainy 33
snowy 33
sunny 33
windy 33
Classroom words
book 24
board 24
bookcase 24
computer 24
desk 24
file cabinet 24
CD 24
notebook 24
pen 24
pencil 24
pencil sharpener 24
plant 24
sit plant 24
stand 29
table 24
trash can 24
Location
between 25
in 25
in the back 25
in the front 25
next to 25
on 25

Unit 3
hungry 45
thirsty 45
Food
apple 42
banana 42
bread 42
broccoli 51
butter 42
cake 53
candy 53
carrot 46

cheese 42
chicken 42
chips 44
chocolate 53
cookie 46
egg 42
fries 44
fruit 49
ground beef 47
ham 41
hamburger 44
ice cream 53
lettuce 42
mayonnaise 42
milk 42
onion 47
orange 42
pear 48
pepper 48
pie 53
potato 42
rice 44
salt 47
sandwich 41
spaghetti 47
taco 44
tomato 42
tunafish 41
turkey 42
vegetables 44
water 42
yogurt 53
Meals
breakfast 43
dinner 43
lunch 43
Containers
and measurements
bag 48
can 48
jar 47
package 47
pound 47
Supermarket
dairy 50
fish 50
meat 50

Unit 4
Clothing
blouse 61
coat 62
dress 62
pants 61
shirt 61

shoes 61
shorts 61
socks 61
sweater 62
Colors
black 68
blue 68
green 68
red 68
white 68
yellow 68
Shopping
cash register 67
receipt 72
sale 73
size 68
small 68
medium 68
large 68
extra large 68
Money
dime 71
dollar 71
nickel 71
penny 71
quarter 71

Unit 5
Places in the community
bank 93
bookstore 93
bus stop 82
clothing store 81
convenience store 81
department store 81
fast food 82
hospital 93
hotel 82
pharmacy 81
post office 93
restaurant 82
shoe store 81
supermarket 81
telephone 82
video store 81
Housing
apartment 84
condominium 85
house 84
mobile home 84
Transportation
car 89
bicycle 89
bus 89
taxi 89

train 89
walk 89
come 89
drive 91
go 89
ride 91
take 91

Directions
go straight 94
stop 94
turn left 94
turn right 94

Unit 6
checkup 110
exercise 110
healthy 110
smoke 110
Parts of Body
arm 102
back 102
ear 103

eye 103
foot 102
hand 102
head 102
leg 102
mouth 103
neck 102
nose 102
Ailments
backache 104
cold 104
cough 104
fever 104
headache 104
runny nose 104
sore throat 110
stomachache 104
Medicine
antacid 108
aspirin 108
cough syrup 108

Unit 7
Occupations
administrative
    assistant 127
bus driver 122
cashier 122
cook 123
custodian 124
doctor 122
employee 127
mail carrier 123
manager 123
nurse 123
receptionist 124
salesperson 122
student 122
teacher 122
worker 128
Work verbs
answer the phone 127
file 128
mop 127

type 127
make change 127
manage employees 127
take breaks 128
talk to customers 127
Evaluations
careful 121
cheerful 121
friendly 121
helpful 121

Unit 8
binder 141
divider 141
goal 150
notebook 145
paper 141
pencil 145
pen 145

Stand Out Basic Grammar Reference

Simple Present

Subject	Verb	Example sentence
I, you, we, they	live take ride walk	I **live** in Mexico. We **take** the bus. You **ride** a bicycle. They **take** a train.
he, she, it	live**s** take**s** ride**s** walk**s**	He **takes** the bus. She **rides** a bicycle.

Simple Present

Subject	Verb	Example sentence
I, you, we, they	eat	I **eat** three meals a day.
he, she, it	sleep**s**	She **sleeps** seven hours a night.

Negative Simple Present

Subject	Verb		Example sentence
I, you, we, they	**don't**	eat	We **don't eat** three meals a day.
he, she, it	**doesn't**	sleep~~s~~	He **doesn't sleep** seven hours a day.

Simple Present: *Be*

Subject	*Be*	Example sentence
I	am	I **am** friendly.
he, she, it	is	She **is** friendly.
we, you, they	are	They **are** friendly.

Simple Present: *Be* (negative)

Subject	*Be* (Negative)	Example sentence
I	am not	I **am not** friendly.
he, she, it	is not	She **is not** friendly.
we, you, they	are not	They **are not** friendly.

Simple Present: *Have*

Subject	*Have*	Example sentence
I, you, we, they	have	I **have** two shirts.
he, she	has	She **has** a dress.

Possessive Adjectives

Subject	Possessive adjective	Example sentence
I	my	**My** phone number is 555-3456.
you	your	**Your** address is 2359 Maple Drive.
he	his	**His** name is Edgar.
she	her	**Her** name is Julie.
we	our	**Our** last name is Perez.
they	their	**Their** teacher is Mr. Jackson.

Prepositions of Location

a. It's **in the front of** the store.

b. It's **in the corner of** the store.

c. It's **in the middle of** the store.

d. It's **in the back of** the store.

e. It's **on the left side of** the store.

f. It's **on the right side of** the store.

How much and *How many*

Question		Answer
How much	(money) is the sweater?	It is $33.00.
How many	coats do you want?	I want three coats.

Yes/No Questions

Question	Answer
Do you buy clothing at a department store?	Yes, I do.
Do you buy food at a supermarket?	No, I don't.
Do you buy shoes at a shoe store?	

Imperatives

	Subject	Verb
Please	~~you~~	read
		open
		let me (look)
		sit down
		stand up

Present Continuous (right now)

Subject	*Be* verb	Base + *ing*	Example sentence
I	am	talking	I **am talking**.
he, she, it	is	sleeping	He **is sleeping**.
we, you, they	are	waiting	They **are waiting**.

Information Questions

Question word	Type of answer
What	information (receptionist)
Where	a place (Johnson Company)
When	a time or day (9–6) (Monday–Friday)
Who	a person (Martin)

Can

Subject	*Can*	Verb (base)	Example sentence
I, you, he, she, it, we, they	can	type	I can type.
		mop	He can mop floors.

Can't

Subject	*Can't*	Verb (base)	Example sentence
I, you, he, she, it, we, they	can't	type	I can't type.
		mop	He can't mop floors.

Affirmative Commands

	Verb		Example sentence
~~You~~	wash	your hands	Wash your hands.
	answer	the phones	Answer the phones.
	type	letters	Type the letters.

Negative Commands

		Verb		Example sentence
~~You~~	don't	wash	your hands	Don't wash your hands.
		answer	the phones	Don't answer the phones.
		type	letters	Don't type the letters.

Stand Out Basic Listening Scripts

PRE-UNIT
CD 1, Track 1, Page P1
A. Listen.
Mrs. Adams: Hello.
Orlando: Hi.

CD 1, Track 2
Mrs. Adams: Goodbye.
Orlando: Bye.

CD 1, Track 3, Page P2
C. Listen and point to the picture. Who is speaking?
Mrs. Adams: Hello. I'm Mrs. Adams.
Orlando: Hi, Mrs. Adams. I'm Orlando. Nice to meet you.
Mrs. Adams: Nice to meet you, too.
Orlando: Bye.
Mrs. Adams: Goodbye.

CD 1, Track 4
Chinh: Hi. I'm Chinh.
Amal: Hello, Chinh. I'm Amal.
Chinh: Nice to meet you.
Amal: Nice to meet you, too.
Chinh: Bye now.
Amal: Bye.

CD 1, Track 5
Page P2, Pronunciation
/mmm/. . . /mmm/. . ./mmm/
I'm a student.
I'm Amal.

CD 1, Track 6, Page P3
E. Listen and repeat. Then, write.
A B C D E F G H I J K L M
N O P Q R S T U V W X Y Z

CD 1, Track 7, Page P4
A. Listen and point. Who is speaking?
Chinh: Hello?
Amal: Hi, Chinh. This is Amal.
Chinh: Hello, Amal. How are you?
Amal: Fine, thanks.

CD 1, Track 8, Page P4
B. Listen and repeat. Point to each number. Then, write all the numbers.
0 1 2 3 4 5 6 7 8 9 10

CD 1, Track 9, Page P5
E. Listen and circle.
1. (714) 555-3450
2. (352) 555-6767
3. (808) 555-3456
4. (915) 555-3455

CD 1, Track 10, Page P7
A. Listen.
Hello, class. Today we will discuss three important things you need to know to participate in class and to learn English. This is a poster. It says you should always listen carefully, read all instructions, and write your name on every sheet of paper. Please repeat these words—listen . . . read . . . write. Again—listen . . . read . . . write. Thank you.

CD 1, Track 11, Page P8
Pronunciation
write . . . write . . . write . . . write
point . . . point . . . point . . . point
repeat . . . repeat . . . repeat . . . repeat

CD 1, Track 12, Page P9
F. Listen and circle the answers.
1. listen **2.** point **3.** write **4.** repeat

CD 1, Track 13, Page P10
G. Listen and bubble in the answers.
1. People use their ears to listen for important information.
2. The teacher is pointing with her finger at the poster in front of the class.
3. I need a paper and a pencil, so I can write a letter.
4. Students, open your mouths and repeat the words clearly.

UNIT 1
CD 1, Track 14, Page 1
A. Listen and point.
Here are three friends of mine from school. He is Amal, she is Chinh, and they are Chinh and Elsa. They are all students in Mrs. Adam's class. Amal is a student, Chinh is a student, and Elsa is a student.

CD 1, Track 15, Page 2
C. Listen and repeat.
I, You, He, She, We, They

I am a student.   She is a student.
You are a student.   We are students.
He is a student.   They are students.

CD 1, Track 16, Page 3
E. Listen.
Chinh: Hi, Satsuki.
Satsuki: Hello, Chinh.
Chinh: Elsa, this is Satsuki. He is a student.
Elsa: Hello, Satsuki. I am a student, too.
Satsuki: Nice to meet you.

CD 1, Track 17, Page 4
A. Read and listen.
Mr. Jackson: Hello, I'm Mr. Jackson. What's your name?
Concepción: My name is Concepción. I'm new in the class.

Mr. Jackson: Nice to meet you. Won't you have a seat?
Concepción: Thank you.
Mr. Jackson: Where are you from, Concepción?
Concepción: I'm from Cuba.
Mr. Jackson: That's great! Welcome to the class.

CD 1, Track 18, Page 5
E. Listen and write.
1.
Mrs. Adams: Hello, I'm Mrs. Adams. What's your name?
Concepción: My name is Concepción. I'm new in the class.
Mrs. Adams: Nice to meet you. Won't you have a seat?
Concepción: Thank you.
Mrs. Adams: Where are you from, Concepción?
Concepción: I'm from Cuba.

CD 1, Track 19
2.
Mrs. Adams: Are you the new student from Lebanon?
Amal: Yes, my name is Amal.
Mrs. Adams: I hope you enjoy our class.
Amal: I will, thank you.

CD 1, Track 20
3.
Mrs. Adams: Hello, Chinh.
Chinh: Hi, Mrs. Adams.
Mrs. Adams: Chinh, where are you from?
Chinh: I'm from Vietnam.

CD 1, Track 21
4.
Mrs. Adams: Hello, Elsa. It is so good to see you today.
Elsa: Yes, I was sick yesterday, but I feel better today.
Mrs. Adams: That's good. I thought you might have gone back to Russia.

CD 1, Track 22
5.
Mrs. Adams: Hello. Welcome to the class. What's your name?
Shiro: I'm Shiro. I came to the United States last week.
Mrs. Adams: Where are you from, Shiro?
Shiro: I'm from Japan.

CD 1, Track 23, Page 6
I. Listen and practice using Shiro, Amal, Elsa, and Chinh.
Mrs. Adams: Hi, Concepción. Where are you from?
Concepción: I'm from Cuba.
Mrs. Adams: Where do you live?
Concepción: I live in Fort Lauderdale, Florida.

CD 1, Track 24, Page 7
A. Listen and write.
   Amal is a student at Fort Lauderdale Adult School. He is single. His birth date is July 3, 1988. He is from Lebanon. Chinh is from Vietnam. Jeff is from the United States. They are married. They got married two years ago. Mirna and

Paul are from Russia. Mirna is a student and wants to speak English better. Mirna and Paul are divorced. They have three children.

CD 1, Track 25, Page 8
D. Listen, circle _Yes_ or _No_, and write.
Hans: Maria, are you single?
Maria: No, I'm married. Hans, are you married?
Hans: No, I'm single. Are Mr. and Mrs. Johnson married?
Maria: Yes, I think so.

CD 1, Track 26, Page 10
C. Listen and point to the addresses.
1. Write down the following address so you can find the location easily. It is 51 Apple Avenue.
2. I need to talk to the resident at 12367 Elm Road. Do you know her?
3. Amal's address is not 51 Apple Avenue. It is different.
4. Let's go to the new adult school. I think the address is 3259 Lincoln Street.

CD 1, Track 27, Page 11
E. Listen and write.
   Amal is a student at Fort Lauderdale Adult School. His address is 8237 Augustin Street, Fort Lauderdale, Florida 33310. Chinh is also a student at Fort Lauderdale Adult School. She lives at 23905 Fin Road, Fort Lauderdale, Florida 33310. Elsa is from Russia. She is a good student. Her address is 23 San Andrew Street, Fort Lauderdale, Florida 33310.

CD 1, Track 28, Page 13
D. Listen to the months and say the number. Listen again and write the months on a sheet of paper.
May   February   August   June   March November
July   September   January   December   April   October

CD 1, Track 29, Page 15
I. Listen and write the dates.
1. My name is Amal. Today is a great day. It's June 25, 2008. I study at school. Next week, July 3 is my birthday. My birth date is July 3, 1988.
2. Elsa is my friend. I see her every day at school. Her birth date is January 12, 1990. That means that she's 19 years old because it's January 12, 2009, today.
3. Chinh: What's the date today?
   Orlando: It's March 2, 2008.
   Chinh: Thanks. It's almost my birthday.
   Orlando: When is your birthday?
   Chinh: March 14!
   Orlando: What year?
   Chinh: 1988.

UNIT 2
CD 1, Track 30, Page 21
B. Listen and practice.
   I want to introduce two new students today. This is Edgar. He is from Senegal. He lives in Sacramento. His phone number is (916) 555-3765.

Meet Julie. She is also a new student. She is from Canada. She lives in Folsom. Her number is (916) 555-4565.

CD 1, Track 31, Page 23
G. Listen and circle.
1. **Mr. Jackson:** Hi, Edgar. I want to introduce you to Susan. She is a friend of mine from class.
   Edgar: Hello, Susan. Nice to meet you.
   Susan: Nice to meet you, too.
2. **Mr. Jackson:** Class, it is my pleasure to tell you about a new student. Please meet Jonathan. He is from Canada. His address and phone number are available if you want to contact him.
3. **Susan:** My name is Susan and this is my good friend, Emanuel. Emanuel is from Israel. We live in Sacramento. Our class is next door.
   John: Nice to meet you. What's your teacher's name?
   Susan: It's Mr. Jackson.

CD 1, Track 32, Page 24
A. Listen and repeat. Point to the picture.
trash can, file cabinets, board, bookcase, plant, door

CD 1, Track 33, Page 24
C. Listen and point.
May I have your attention, please? Class, I want to give you a quick tour of the classroom and talk about some class rules. Look around and see if you can find the items I will describe to you. Of course, the board is in the front of the class. Here, I write important information. If you need a pencil sharpener, please use the electric one during group work, and not when I am talking. We can move tables in the classroom when it is necessary to do group work. If you need to borrow a book, go to the bookcase. Please don't leave trash around the room. Use the trash can whenever possible. Finally, we will use the computers in the back of the room twice a week. I hope you know that I don't want you sitting in your chairs all the time. You will have many opportunities to get up and walk around. Also, we will keep the door closed during class, so you can concentrate on your work in the class. Any questions?

CD 1, Track 34, Page 27
A. Listen and point.
All the students work hard in Mr. Jackson's English class. Two students are talking in the back of the room about their homework. One student is writing at his desk. Shiro is at his desk, too. He is listening to a tape. Julie is reading. She is a good student.

CD 1, Track 35, Page 30
A. Read and listen.
Shiro has a busy schedule. He has English class at 9 A.M. At 12:00 he eats lunch. He goes to class again at 1:00 in the afternoon. He has pronunciation class. He goes to work at 4 P.M.

CD 1, Track 36, Page 32
F. Listen and write.
Cameron: Hi, Julie. How are you?
Julie: Fine, thanks.
Cameron: What is your schedule today?
Julie: I have English class at 9:00, work at 11:00, lunch at 1:30 and finally, I go to bed at 10:30 tonight.
Cameron: I see you are very busy. Maybe we could have lunch at 1:30.
Julie: That would be great!

CD 1, Track 37, Page 32
G. Listen and read.
Julie: When's English class?
Mr. Jackson: It's at 9:00.
Julie: What time is it now?
Mr. Jackson: It's 7:30.

CD 1, Track 38, Page 33
A. Listen and repeat.
windy, cloudy, foggy, rainy, snowy, cold, hot, sunny

CD 1, Track 39, Page 33
B. Listen and write.
This is Express Weather from Miami, Florida. We are happy to bring you the latest weather throughout the world. Let's start with Havana, Cuba. It's hot today in Havana with a temperature of 98 degrees. In Tokyo, Japan, it is cloudy and unusually cold for this time of year. In Patagonia, Chile, be careful when driving. It's very windy today. Moving along to the north of us in Montreal, Canada, the bitter cold is keeping everyone indoors. Yes, it's very cold. In Lisbon, Portugal, it's foggy at the docks and shipping is hampered. In Mombasa, Kenya, it's rainy and the rain will continue for several days.

CD 1, Track 40, Page 34, Pronunciation
How's the weather? How is the weather?
How's the weather in Havana today?

How's the weather? How is the weather?
How's the weather? It's hot today.

UNIT 3
CD 1, Track 41, Page 41
A. Listen.
Andre: The food looks good!
Silvina: Yes, it does.
Andre: What are you eating?
Silvina: A turkey sandwich.

CD 1, Track 42, Page 42
C. Listen and point.

a. milk	**b.** water	**c.** eggs	**d.** chicken
e. bananas	**f.** bread	**g.** cheese	**h.** turkey
i. tomatoes	**j.** lettuce	**k.** apples	**l.** oranges
m. potatoes	**n.** mayonnaise	**o.** butter	

CD 1, Track 43, Page 44
B. Listen and read.
Saul: I'm hungry.
Chen: Me, too.
Saul: What's for dinner?
Chen: chicken and vegetables

CD 1, Track 44, Page 46
F. Read and listen.
carrots, oranges, apples, chips, cookies, milk, water

CD 1, Track 45, Page 46
G. Listen and write the snack.
1. **A:** I'm hungry.
   B: Me, too. I really need something healthy.
   A: Carrots are always good, and healthy, too.
CD 1, Track 46
2. **A:** I'm thirsty.
   B: Can I get you anything?
   A: Maybe some water would help.
   B: I'll get it right away.
CD 1, Track 47
3. **A:** Do you have anything to eat?
   B: Sure, but what do you want?
   A: I don't know. I'm very hungry.
   B: How about an apple?
   A: Thanks.
CD 1, Track 48
4. **A:** My sister is very hungry. She needs to eat.
   B: What can I get her?
   A: Do you have any oranges?
   B: I'll get her one.

CD 1, Track 49, Page 47
C. Listen and circle.
1. **Omar:** There is so much we need at the store.
   Maria: What do you mean? What do we need?
   Omar: We need a package of spaghetti, for one thing.
   Maria: OK, I'll write it on the list. What else?
CD 1, Track 50
2. **Omar:** Well, let's see . . . We need at least one pound
   of chicken for dinner tonight.
   Maria: Are you sure one pound is enough?
   Omar: Yes. We have a pound in the refrigerator.
   Maria: I'm adding it to the list. What else?

CD 1, Track 51
3. **Omar:** We need a package of cheese for sandwiches.
   Maria: No, we don't. I have three packages in the
   refrigerator.
   Omar: Oh, I didn't see them.
   Maria: What else?
CD 1, Track 52
4. **Omar:** We need a jar of mayonnaise for the sandwiches.
   Maria: I don't like mayonnaise, but I will put it on the
   list for you.
   Omar: Thanks!

CD 1, Track 53, Page 48
D. Read the chart. Listen. Repeat.

jar	jars
can	cans
bag	bags
package	packages
pound	pounds

CD 1, Track 54, Page 50
A. Listen and point.

oranges	apples	pears	bananas	strawberries
carrots	tomatoes	potatoes	broccoli	lettuce
chicken	ground beef	turkey	fish	cheese	yogurt

CD 1, Track 55, Page 51
F. What does Yoshi want? Listen and write.
Amadeo: Yoshi, I'm going to the supermarket. What
do you want?
Yoshi: Um, I want some oranges, apples, and strawberries.
Amadeo: Is that all?
Yoshi: No. I think I want some yogurt, cheese, and eggs, too.
Amadeo: OK, is that it?
Yoshi: No. Get me some potatoes, fish, and water.
Amadeo: Anything else.
Yoshi: No, that's it.
Amadeo: OK, let me read it back to you. You want oranges,
apples, strawberries, yogurt, cheese, eggs, potatoes, fish,
and water.
Yoshi: Yep, that's all!

CD 1, Track 56, Page 53
**A. Circle the desserts you like to eat. Then, listen
and repeat.**
  cake, pie, ice cream, yogurt, cookies, bar of chocolate,
  bag of candy

CD 1, Track 57, Page 53
B. Listen and point to the desserts in Exercise A.
1. **Man:** What dessert would you like?
   Woman: Well, I really like chocolate, but the apple pie
   looks good, too.
CD 1, Track 58
2. **Woman:** Just wait until you see what's for dessert.
   Man: What is it?
   Woman: I have cake and cookies. We also have some
   candy for later.
CD 1, Track 59
3. **Man:** Let me take you out and buy you a special dessert.
   Woman: That sounds great. What dessert?
   Man: I don't know. What do you want?
   Woman: How about ice cream or pie?
   Man: OK. We could also have cookies if you want.

CD 1, Track 60, Page 53
C. Listen. Write what Maria likes.
   Maria likes dessert. She especially likes cake. She also
   likes cookies. She eats dessert after every meal.

UNIT 4
CD 1, Track 61, Page 61
A. Listen.
Salesperson: May I help you?
Maria: Yes, I want a shirt, pants, a sweater, and shoes.

CD 1, Track 62, Page 62
D. Listen and write the number of the conversation.
1.
Saleswoman: Excuse me. Can I help you?
Customer: Yes, I need a few things, but I don't see anything here that will fit.
Saleswoman: I think this blouse would be perfect for you. The colors go great with your eyes.
Customer: Do you really think so? Maybe you're right.
2.
Son: Mom, can you buy some socks when you are out? I need them for basketball practice.
Mother: Sure, son, I will buy you three pairs.
3.
Man 1: This shirt is way too big for me. I really need to be more careful when I go shopping.
Man 2: That's why I ask my wife to buy shirts for me. She is a much better shopper than me.
4.
Wife: I have three pairs of pants in my closet, but I don't want to wear any of them.
Husband: Why don't you where the blue pair? They look great on you.
5.
Woman 1: It is so cold out. I wish I brought my coat.
Woman 2: You're right. Let's get inside as soon as possible.
6.
Daughter: Mom, can I go to the park for a while with Becky?
Mother: Yes, dear, but it is getting cold. Please put on a sweater. Then, I won't worry.
7.
Son: Dad, will you play basketball with me? I think I need some help.
Father: OK, let me get changed. I need to find my shorts.
8.
Husband: Is this a formal dinner we are going to?
Wife: I think so. I'm wearing a dress so you should wear something nice.

CD 1, Track 63, Page 64
A. Listen and point.
Men's   Women's   Children   Teen Boys'
Teen Girls'   Fitting Room

CD 1, Track 64, Page 65
E. Listen and practice.
A: Can you help me?
B: Sure. What can I do for you?
A: Where's the fitting room?
B: It's in the back of the store.
A: Thank you.

CD 1, Track 65, Page 66
F. Listen and point.
Point to the front right corner of the store.
Point to the middle of the store.
Point to the back left corner of the store.
Point to the right side of the store.
Point to the back of the store.
Point to the front of the store.
Point to the back right corner of the store.
Point to the front left corner of the store.

CD 1, Track 66, Page 66
G. Listen and write the sections in the picture.
1. **A:** Excuse me, where is the fitting room?
   B: It's in the back left corner of the store.
   A: Thanks!
2. **A:** Can I help you?
   B: I'm looking for the women's section.
   A: The women's section is in the front right corner of the store.
3. **A:** I'm looking for the children's section.
   B: The children's section is in the middle of the store. Do you need any help?
   A: No, thank you.
4. **A:** Excuse me. Where is the men's section?
   B: It's in the front left side of the store.
   A: Thanks.
5. **A:** I need help.
   B: Yes, what can I do for you?
   A: I need to find my sister. She said she would be in the teen girls' section.
   B: The teen girls' section is in the back right.

CD 1, Track 67, Page 67
B. Listen and read.
Salesperson: Can I help you?
Yusuf: Yes, I want a shirt.
Salesperson: What color do you like—white, blue, or red?
Yusuf: I don't know, maybe blue.

CD 1, Track 68, Page 68
C. Listen and repeat.
red, yellow, blue, green, white, black

CD 1, Track 69, Page 68
D. Listen and point to the clothing items.
Salesperson: We have many sizes and colors in our store. For example, in this shirt, we have two extra-large blue shirts.
Yusuf: I don't need that size. Do you have any large white shirts?
Salesperson: Sure, we have one in the back. I can get it for you.
Yusuf: OK, and while you're at it, could you get me a medium green shirt for my brother?
Salesperson: OK, but are you sure he might not want a small yellow shirt? We have three of those on sale.
Yusuf: Yes, I'm sure.

CD 1, Track 70, Page 70
A. Listen and read the cash registers.
1.
Cashier: Let's see. You want this comb. That's $1.00.
Tien: $1.00?
Cashier: That's right.
Tien: OK, here you go.
2.
Cashier: OK, that's one red t-shirt.
Tien: How much is it?
Cashier: That's $6.25 with tax.
3.
Cashier: Let's see. The shorts are $10.41.
Tien: OK, do you have change?
Cashier: Sure.
Tien: Thanks!

CD 1, Track 71, Page 71
D. Listen and read with your teacher.

a dollar bill / a dollar coin	one dollar
a quarter	twenty-five cents
a dime	ten cents
a nickel	five cents
a penny	one cent

CD 1, Track 72, Page 72
F. Listen and Write
1.
Salesman: Can I help you?
Yusuf: Yes, I want this pair of pants.
Salesman: Great. Step this way.
Yusuf: How much are they?
Salesman: They're $32.50.
CD 1, Track 73
2.
Salesman: Can I help you?
Yusuf: Yes, I want a shirt. This one looks good.
Salesman: That's $24.50.
CD 1, Track 74
3.
Salesman: Can I help you?
Maria: Yes, I need a pair of shoes for work.
Salesman: Here is a nice pair.
Maria: How much are they?
Salesman: They are $44.00.
CD 1, Track 75
4.
Salesman: Can I help you?
Yusuf: Yes, I want a pair of shorts.
Salesman: Great. Step this way.
Yusuf: How much are they?
Salesman: They are $18.00.
CD 1, Track 76
5.
Salesman: Can I help you?
Maria: Yes, I need a dress for a party.
Salesman: What color are you looking for?
Maria: Something for the summer.

Salesman: How about this one?
Maria: That's beautiful. How much is it?
Salesman: It's $82.50.
CD 1, Track 77
6.
Saleswoman: Can I help you?
Maria: Yes, I'm looking for a blouse.
Saleswoman: What color are you looking for?
Maria: Maybe white.
Saleswoman: How about this one?
Maria: That's pretty. How much is it?
Saleswoman: It's $22.50.

CD 1, Track 78, Page 73
A. Read, listen, and write.
   Here at Adel's Clothing Emporium, we have great sales. Come in and see for yourself. Men's shirts in all sizes are only $22.50. You will be happy to see women's dresses in sizes 6 to 12 are only $33.00. We have men's sweaters on sale for $33.00. Men's pants are only $28.00 this week. Women's shoes are now only $24. Save $4.00! Blouses are a bargain at $18.00! We will be waiting for you. Remember Adel's Clothing Emporium for great savings!

UNIT 5
CD 2, Track 1, Page 81
A. Listen and point.
1. clothing store
2. shoe store
3. pharmacy
4. supermarket
5. video store
6. convenience store
7. department store

CD 2, Track 2, Page 81
B. Listen and write the number of the conversation.
1.
A: We need to go to the store.
B: Why? What do we need?
A: We need lots of things. We need milk, apples, and bread.
B: Then, we need to go to the supermarket right away.
A: You said it!
CD 2, Track 3
2.
A: My feet hurt.
B: It's those shoes you're wearing.
A: These things are old, but I love them.
B: I think if we were to go to a shoe store, you would feel a lot better.
A: OK, let's go.
CD 2, Track 4
3.
A: I need a new dress for the party.
B: What size do you wear?
A: I wear a size 9.
B: I think the clothing store on the corner has a good selection.
A: Really? That's great. Let's go.

CD 2, Track 5

4.

A: We need some medicine.

B: Yes, I know. We need to buy some aspirin and cough syrup.

A: Sounds like a good idea. Let's get some bandages, too.

B: OK. Let's go to the pharmacy down the street.

CD 2, Track 6

5.

A: There is a new movie on DVD. You've got to see it.

B: Is it good?

A: Yeah, it's great.

B: OK, let's rent it. The video store is still open.

CD 2, Track 7, Page 82

C. Listen and point to the signs.

1. Find the hotel.

2. Find the restaurant.

3. Find the fast-food restaurant.

4. Find the clothing store.

5. Find the shoe store.

6. Find the pharmacy.

7. Find the video store.

8. Find the bus stop.

9. Find the telephone.

CD 2, Track 8, Page 84

B. Listen and practice.

A: Where do you live?

B: I live on First Street.

A: Do you live in a house or an apartment?

B: I live in a house.

CD 2, Track 9, Page 85

E. Listen and write.

1. I think that you will be very happy with our special this week. This is a fine three-bedroom house with new floors in a beautiful neighborhood. Please come and see it. It's on Parker Street.

2. My family and I live in a three-bedroom home in the city. It is on a big lot. We enjoy our mobile home. We have many friends who live in the park.

3. There is a great rental on Parker Avenue. I think it is under $1,000 a month. It is a two-bedroom apartment and there is a community pool.

CD 2, Track 10, Page 86

F. Listen and read.

1. I'm Chen. I'm from China. I live in a house. I live on First Street in Alpine City.

2. I'm Latifa. I'm from Saudi Arabia. I live in an apartment. I live in Casper Town on Parker Avenue.

3. I'm Natalia. I'm from Guatemala. I live in a condominium in Alpine City on First Street.

CD 2, Track 11, Page 87

B. Listen and read.

Chen: Do you drive to school?

Latifa: No, I don't. I take the bus.

Chen: How much is it?

Latifa: It's 75 cents.

CD 2, Track 12, Page 90

A. Listen and write.

1. I'm James. I'm from the U.S. I live in a house. I take the bus to school.

2. I'm Nga. I'm from Vietnam. I live in a house. I ride a bicycle to school.

3. I'm Carina. I'm from Cuba. I live in an apartment. I drive to school.

CD 2, Track 13, Page 94

D. Listen and repeat.

stop, go straight, turn right, turn left

CD 2, Track 14, Page 95

I. Listen and read.

Carina: Excuse me, where's American Café?

Nga: It's on Perry Avenue.

Carina: Can you give me directions?

Nga: Yes. Go straight on First Street. Turn right on Perry Avenue. It's next to Pete's Burgers.

CD 2, Track 15, Page 95

J. Listen and follow the directions. Number the locations 1-4.

1. Go straight. Turn right on Perry Avenue. It's next to Pete's Burgers.

2. Turn right on Hampton Street. Turn left on Second Street. It's next to Ned's Shoes.

3. Turn right on Hampton Street. It's next to El Marco Restaurant.

4. Go straight. Turn right on Perry Avenue. Turn right on Second Street. It's next to Big's Foods.

UNIT 6

CD 2, Track 16, Page 101

B. Listen and write.

My name is Guillermo. I live in Chicago. I am 61 years old. I see the doctor once a year for a checkup. I'm very healthy.

CD 2, Track 17, Page 103

G. Listen and practice the conversation.

Doctor: Please sit down.

Guillermo: OK.

Doctor: Please open your mouth and say, "Ah."

Guillermo: Ah.

CD 2, Track 18, Page 104

A. Listen and repeat.

headache, backache, stomachache
cold and runny nose, cough and sore throat, fever

CD 2, Track 19, Page 104

B. Listen and point.

1.

Doctor: It is good to see you.

Woman: It's good to see you, too.

Doctor: What's the matter today?
Woman: I have a terrible stomachache. Maybe I ate something bad yesterday.

CD 2, Track 20
2.
Doctor: You look like you are in a lot of pain today.
Man: I sure am. Every day I get these terrible headaches. What can I do about it?
Doctor: For headaches, we usually prescribe pain relievers, but maybe we should check this out with some tests.
Man: Thanks, Doctor.

CD 2, Track 21
3.
Doctor: How can I help you?
Man: I think I have a high fever.
Doctor: Let's check it out.
Man: Thanks, Doctor. I hope I'm not too sick.

CD 2, Track 22
4.
Doctor: You must be feeling terrible.
Woman: I sure am. I think I've only got a cold, but it is causing so many problems.
Doctor: I know you want to go to work, but sometimes, even with a cold, you need to take it easy for a few days.
Woman: I guess you're right. I just hate staying home!

CD 2, Track 23
5.
Doctor: Can I help you?
Man: Yes, I can hardly move.
Doctor: What seems to be the trouble?
Man: I have a terrible backache.

CD 2, Track 24
6.
Doctor: How are you feeling today?
Woman: Not very well. I think I have a cold. I have a bad cough and a sore throat.
Doctor: Let me take a look.
Woman: Thanks, Doctor.

CD 2, Track 25, Page 106
F. Listen and bubble in the correct answer.
1. Maritza is a good student. She can't come to school today because she has a headache. I hope she comes back tomorrow.

CD 2, Track 26
2. Shan works all day and comes to school at night. He isn't at school today. He called me and told me he would be out because he had a fever of around 102 degrees. I hope he is all right and will get better soon.

CD 2, Track 27
3. Hi, John! This is your teacher, Rob. I hear you are having a hard time with a cold and a runny nose. It's no fun to be sick. Get well soon! Bye.

CD 2, Track 28
4. Anakiya is new in the United States. She arrived Tuesday. I hope she will be OK. She is already sick. She has a fever.

CD 2, Track 29, Page 107
A. Read, listen, and write the missing words.
Doctor: I'm a little late. I will be there soon. What patients do we have today? Oh, and can you give me their numbers, too? I might want to call a few before I get to the office.
Nurse: No problem, Doctor. Let's see. Julio Rodriguez has an appointment at 3:30. He has a headache. His number is 555-1395. Huong Pham is coming in at 4:00. He has a high fever. His phone is 555-3311. Richard Price has an appointment at 4:30. He has a stomachache. His number is 555-2323. Mele Ikahihifo has a sore throat. She's coming in at 5:00. You can reach her at 555-5511. Fred Wharton's number is 555-9764. He has a cold. Ayumi Tanaka is coming in at 6:00 with a backache. Her number is 555-8765.
Doctor: Thanks.

CD 2, Track 30, Page 110
A. Read and listen.
Health Tips
We are happy you are a patient of Dr. Ramsey. Our goal is to help you stay healthy. Follow these suggestions and you will be healthier.
Do's: Sleep! Sleep seven to eight hours a day. Eat! Eat three good meals a day. Exercise! Walk, run, or exercise 30 minutes every day. See the doctor! See the doctor once a year for a checkup.
Don'ts: Don't smoke.
For emergency appointments, call 720-555-4311.

CD 2, Track 31, Page 111
C. Listen and read Huong's story. Why is Huong healthy?
   I'm healthy. I exercise one hour every day. I eat breakfast, lunch, and dinner. I don't eat a lot of candy. I don't smoke. I sleep seven hours every night.

CD 2, Track 32, Page 113
B. Listen to the conversation. What words do you hear first? Write 1-5.

Doctor: I'm a little late. I will be there in ten minutes. How many patients are there?
Receptionist: There are four. They are all waiting. Mrs. Hill and Mrs. Johnson are talking, and Guillermo Espinosa is reading a magazine. Mr. Masters is sleeping in a chair.
Doctor: What are you doing?
Receptionist: I'm answering the phone and writing patient information in their files.
Doctor: OK, I'll see you in a few minutes.

UNIT 7
CD 2, Track 33, Page 121
B. Listen and read.
   My name is Emilio. I live in Dallas, Texas. I have a new job. I'm a cashier at Ultra Supermarket on Broadway! This is a picture of my class.

CD 2, Track 34, Page 122
D. Listen and repeat the words.

cashier   doctor   bus driver   student
salesperson   teacher

CD 2, Track 35, Page 124
A. Listen.

1. Hello, I'm Isabel. I have a great job. I am a receptionist. I work for the Johnson Company and my supervisor's name is Martin. I work from 9:00 A.M. to 6:00 P.M., Monday through Friday. I take a one-hour lunch break at 12:00.
2. My name is Colleen. I am the manager of Freedman's Foods. My supervisor is Amelia. I work Wednesday through Sunday from 2:00 P.M. to 10:00 P.M. I take a one-hour break at 6:00.
3. I'm Fred. My friends call me Freddy. I work late at night. I work from 10:00 P.M. to 7:00 A.M., Sunday to Friday. I'm a custodian at America Bank. My supervisor's name is Mary.

CD 2, Track 36, Page 124
B. Listen and write the names of the people from Exercise A.

1.
Manager: Please take care of the customer over there.
Employee: OK. You are the boss.
Manager: Oh, and please write down any problems she is having.
Employee: I can do that.
Manager: You can go home after you take care of those two things.
Employee: Thanks!
2.
Custodian: Excuse me, I need to mop under your desk.
Coworker: OK, I'll move for a few minutes.
Custodian: Thanks. I need to mop the whole bank every day.
3.
Manager: My name is Martin. I am your new supervisor.
Receptionist: Nice to meet you, Martin.
Manager: Nice to meet you, too. When do you come to work?
Receptionist: I work from 9:00 A.M. to 6:00 P.M. every weekday.

CD 2, Track 37, Page 126
I. Listen. Fill in the chart about Tan, Maria, and Alfredo. What does Tan do? When and where does he work?

My name is Tan. I have a great job. I work late at night and sleep during the day. I'm a custodian. I start work at 3:00 P.M. I work at a school.

CD 2, Track 38
What does Maria do? When and where does she work?

My name is Maria. I'm a manager at a restaurant. I work Monday through Friday. I work with customers and all the employees.

CD 2, Track 39
What does Alfredo do? When and where does he work?

My name is Alfredo. I'm a nurse. I work at a hospital. I take care of patients and help the doctors on the fifth floor. I start work at 6:00 P.M.

CD 2, Track 40, Page 127
A. Listen and point.

1. Receptionists have many responsibilities. They file and talk to customers. They also answer the phone.
2. Administrative assistants are very important. They do many things. One of the important things they do is type letters. Some secretaries can type more than 100 words a minute.
3. A salesperson is important. He or she talks to customers and answers their questions.
4. Custodians work in many different places. The custodian at the elementary school mops the floor, cleans the rooms, and helps the teachers.

CD 2, Track 41, Page 127
B. What do they do? Listen and write.

1. An administrative assistant has important responsibilities. He or she types letters, for one thing.
2. Custodians work in many different places. The custodian at an elementary school mops floors.
3. Receptionists have many responsibilities. For example, a receptionist in an office answers phones.
4. A salesperson is important. He or she talks to customers and does many other things.
5. Cashiers are usually in the front of a store or business. A cashier in a supermarket makes change as well as many other things.
6. A manager is responsible for seeing that all goes well in a business. He or she supervises other employees.
7. A nurse in a hospital helps the doctors as much as possible.

CD 2, Track 42, Page 131
E. Listen and circle.

I evaluated Chan Chin today. He is a very good worker and I think he is a good employee because, overall, his attitude is very good.

He is always happy and cheerful. This is important because the customers see this and it helps them to feel good about our store. Chan is not always helpful, though, because he is new and doesn't know very much about the job. In time, he will get better. Chan and Jim are not careful enough. They were responsible for the lamp being broken in the lighting section. I have asked Chan to work on being more careful around the displays. Chan has a good attitude. He talks to the customers and is very friendly. Overall, I am happy with Chan's work.

CD 2, Track 43, Page 133
A. Listen and point.

1. Don't smoke.   2. Wash your hands.   3. File the papers.
4. Fred, please answer the phones.   5. Fred, please type these letters.   6. Don't eat in the office.

UNIT 8
CD 2, Track 44, Page 141
A. Listen and repeat.
binder, dividers, sheets of lined paper

CD 2, Track 45, Page 142
C. Listen and bubble in.
1.
Liang: The teacher wants us to make special binders to study after school is finished.
Octavio: Yes, I know. We have to go to the store and buy some things. I don't think it will be expensive.
Liang: We need binders first.
Octavio: What size do we need?
Liang: I think we need 1½" binders.
Octavio: That sounds right. They shouldn't be too big.
2.
Liang: We need dividers, too.
Octavio: What are dividers?
Liang: You know, the heavy paper to make sections in your binder.
Octavio: Oh, yeah. How many do we need?
Liang: We need a set of five dividers.
3.
Octavio: What else do we need?
Liang: We need paper for each section.
Octavio: How many sheets do we need?
Liang: Two hundred sheets, I think.
Octavio: That sounds right.

CD 2, Track 46, Page 144
B. Listen to the conversation and practice.
Customer: Excuse me, how much are the dividers?
Salesperson: They are $2.00 for a set of five.
Customer: Thanks. I need one set please.

CD 2, Track 47, Page 145
C. Listen and repeat.
I need a box of pencils.
I need a two-inch binder.
I need a set of five colored dividers.
I need a package of paper.
I need a box of ballpoint pens.
I need a notebook.

CD 2, Track 48, Page 147
B. Listen to the conversation. Write.
Linda: Excuse me, where is Reams Office Supplies?
Officer: It's on First Street.
Linda: On First Street?
Officer: Yes, go straight on this street. Turn right on Main Street and left on First. It's next to the video store.
Linda: Thanks.

CD 2, Track 49, Page 150
B. Listen and check Carina's three goals.
I have many goals. There are a lot of things that I want to accomplish. Right now, I'm focusing on daily goals. First, I need to exercise every day. I want to get up early and exercise one hour a day. It's important to be physically fit. I suppose that it's important to be prepared for school every day, too, so I'm going to study a lot. I plan to study for one hour every day, even if I'm tired after work. I need to learn English, and studying will help me do it faster. Somehow, I need to get plenty of sleep, too. Right now, I only sleep six hours a night, but my goal is to get eight hours of sleep. I hope I can do it. That's my goal. With all these goals, I will be healthy and have great success at school.

CD 2, Track 50, Page 153
A. Listen and point.
Teachers and students share many duties, or responsibilities. Among them are several very important things. For example, teachers and students should come to class on time. Students don't like to come early and find that the teacher is late. The teacher should come with a prepared lesson every day. That's also very important. Students have more confidence in a teacher who is prepared. The teacher teaches the students, but students can also teach each other. Students should study at home. There is a lot that they can study. For example, they can study new words at home. Sometimes the teacher gives homework. Students who do their homework learn English faster.

Photo Credits

Front Matter:
Page iv: © Courtney Sabbagh

Pre-Unit:
Page P2: Left: © David Young-Wolff/PhotoEdit; Right: © Mark Segal/Index Stock Imagery
Page P4: Left: © David Young-Wolff/PhotoEdit; Center: © Hemera Photo Objects; Right: © Mark Segal/Index Stock Imagery
Page P5: Left: © Photos.com/RF; Middle Left: © IndexOpen/RF; Middle Right: © Photos.com/RF; Right: © Photos.com/RF

Unit 1:
Page 5: Left: © David Young-Wolff/PhotoEdit; Right: © Mark Segal/Index Stock Imagery
Page 8: Top Left: © Photos.com/RF; Top Right: © ImageSource/SuperStock; Bottom: © BananaStock/Alamy
Page 11: Top: © David Young-Wolff/PhotoEdit; Center: © Mark Segal/Index Stock Imagery; Bottom: © Bob Mahoney/The Image Works
Page 17: © David Young-Wolff/PhotoEdit
Page 18: Top Left: © Susanne Wegele/Stock4B/Getty Images; Bottom Left: © VStock/Alamy; Top Right: © IndexOpen/RF; Bottom Right: © Mark Segal/Index Stock Imagery; © Bob Mahoney/The Image Works

Unit 2:
Page 27: © Hemera Photo Objects
Page 28: #1: © Hemera Photo Objects; #2: © Hemera Photo Objects; #3: © Hemera Photo Objects; #4: © Hemera Photo Objects; #5: © Hemera Photo Objects; #6: © Karen Bleier/AFP/Getty Images
Page 29: Left: © imagewerks/Getty Images; Right: © Photos.com/RF
Page 33: Top Left: © Purestock/Getty Images; Top Right: © Photos.com/RF; Center Left: © Pete Seaward/Stone/Getty Images; Center Right: © Paulo Magalhaes/Riser/Getty Images; Bottom Left: © blickwinkel/Alamy; Bottom Right: © B2M Productions/Digital Vision/Getty Images
Page 34: Top Left: © Purestock/Getty Images; Top Right: © Photos.com/RF; Center Left: © Pete Seaward/Stone/Getty Images; Center Right: © Paulo Magalhaes/Riser/Getty Images; Bottom Left: © blickwinkel/Alamy; Bottom Right: © B2M Productions/Digital Vision/Getty Images
Page 35: Left: © Stockbyte/Getty Images; Center Left: © Photo Objects/RF; Center Right: © Photos.com/RF; Right: © Photos.com/RF
Page 36: Top Left: © Darrin Klimek/Riser/Getty Images; Bottom Right: © Photos.com/RF
Page 38: #1: © Photos.com/RF; #2: © Photos.com/RF; #3: © Photos.com/RF; #4: © Photos.com/RF

Unit 3:
Page 44: Top Left: © Photos.com/RF; Top Right: © IndexOpen/RF; Bottom Left: © IndexOpen/RF; Bottom Center Left: © IndexOpen/RF; Bottom Center Right: © Great American Stock/Index Stock; Right: © Photos.com/RF

Page 46: Top Left: © Photos.com/RF; Top Center Left: © Photos.com/RF; Top Center Right: © Photos.com/RF; Top Right: © Foodcollection/Getty Images; Bottom Left: © Photos.com/RF; Bottom Center: © IndexOpen/RF; Bottom Right: © D. Hurst/Alamy
Page 48: Top: © Bill Boch/FoodPix/Jupiterimages; 2nd from top: © Chloe Johnson/Alamy; 3rd from top: © Foodcollection/Getty Images; 4th from top: © Burke/Triolo Productions/FoodPix/Jupiterimages; 5th from top: © Andersen Ross/Digital Vision/Getty Images; Bottom Left: © Photos.com/RF; Bottom Right: © Photos.com/RF
Page 49: Top Left column, top to bottom: © Photos.com/RF; © Photos.com/RF; © Photos.com/RF; © IndexOpen/RF; Top Right column, top to bottom: © Photos.com/RF; © Photos.com/RF; © Photos.com/RF; © Photos.com/RF; Bottom Left: © Photos.com/RF and Photos.com/RF; Bottom Center Left: © Photos.com/RF and Photos.com/RF; Bottom Center Right: © Photos.com/RF and Photos.com/RF; Bottom Right: © IndexOpen/RF and Photos.com/RF
Page 53: Top row, left to right: © Hemera Photos Objects; © Hemera Photo Objects; © IndexOpen/RF; D. Hurst/Alamy; Bottom Left: © Hemera Photo Objects; Bottom Center: © Hemera Photo Objects; Bottom Right: © IndexOpen/RF
Page 56: Top Left: © Photos.com/RF; Top Center Left: © Photos.com/RF; Top Center: © Hemera Photo Objects; Top Center Right: © Photos.com/RF; Right: © Photo Objects/RF; Bottom Left: © IndexOpen/RF, Photo Objects/RF; Bottom Center Left: © Foodcollection/Getty Images; Bottom Center: © Photos.com/RF; Bottom Center Right: © Hemera Photo Objects; Bottom Right: © Photos.com/RF

Unit 4:
Page 62: Top Left: © Photo Objects/RF; Top Center: © Photo Objects/RF; Top Right: © Thomas Northcut/Photodisc/Getty Images; Center Left: © IndexOpen/RF; Center: © Jack Hollingsworth/Blend Images/Getty Images; Center Right: © Photo Objects/RF; Bottom Left: © D. Hurst/Alamy; Bottom Center: © Photos.com/RF
Page 70: Left: © Photos.com/RF; Center Top: © Photos.com/RF; Center Middle: © Photo Objects/RF; Center Bottom: © Photodisc/Getty Images; Right Top: © Photos.com/RF, Right Bottom: © Photodisc/Getty Images
Page 71: Top: © Photos.com/RF; Coins, left to right: © Photos.com/RF; © Photodisc/Getty Images; © Photodisc/Getty Images; © Photodisc/Getty Images; © Photodisc/Getty Images; Answer A: Top: © Photos.com/RF; Bottom: © Photo Objects/RF; Right: © Photodisc/Getty Images; Answer B: Top Left: © Photo Objects/RF; Top Right: © Photo Objects/RF; Bottom Left: © Photos.com/RF; Bottom Right: © Photodisc/Getty Images; Answer C: © Photodisc/Getty Images

Page 72: Top Left: © Photos.com/RF; Center Left: © Photos.com/RF; Bottom Left: © Photos.com/RF; Top Right: © Photos.com/RF; Center Right: © IndexOpen/RF; Bottom Right: © Jack Hollingsworth/Blend Images/Getty Images
Page 76: Top Left: © Photo Objects/RF; Top Center: © Photos.com/RF; © Top Right: © Thomas Northcut/Photodisc/Getty Images; Center Left: © Photo Objects/RF; © Photos.com/RF; Center Right: © IndexOpen/RF; Bottom Left: © Jack Hollingsworth/Blend Images/Getty Images; Bottom Right: © D. Hurst/Alamy

Unit 5:
Page 86: Left: © Kevin Peterson/Photodisc/Getty Images; Center: © Hemera Photodisc; Right: © Hemera Photodisc
Page 87: Left: © Francesco Bittichesu/Photonica/Getty Images; Right: © IndexOpen/RF
Page 88: Top Left: © Francesco Bittichesu/Photonica//Getty Images; Center Left: © IndexOpen/RF; Bottom Left: ©Mitchell Funk/Photographer's Choice/Getty Images; Top Right: © Photos.com/RF; Bottom Right: © Photo Objects/RF
Page 90: Left: © John A. Rizzo/Stockbyte/Getty Images; Center: © Michael Newman/PhotoEdit; Right: © Ryan McVay/Photodisc/Getty Images
Page 97: Left: © MIXA Co., Ltd./Alamy; Right: © Photodisc/Getty Images

Unit 6:
Page 104: Top Left: © BananaStock Ltd.; Top Center: © BananaStock Ltd.; Top Right: © MIXA/Getty Images; Bottom Left: © BananaStock Ltd.; Bottom Center: © Donn Thompson/DK Stock/Getty Images; Bottom Right: ©Tom Le Goff/Digital Vision/Getty Images
Page 111: © Amos Morgan/Photodisc/Getty Images
Page 112: Left: © © Mark Anderson/Rubberball/Alamy; Center: © Amy Eckert/UpperCut Images/Getty Images; Right: © Photos.com/RF

Unit 7:
Page 124: Top Left: © IndexOpen/RF; Top Right: © IndexOpen/RF; Bottom Left: © Mark Anderson/RubberBall/Alamy
Page 126: © Digital Vision/Getty Images
Page 127: Top Left: © IndexOpen/RF; Bottom Left: © Photos.com/RF; Top Right: © IndexOpen/RF; Bottom Right: © Mark Anderson/RubberBall/Alamy
Page 128: Left: © Keith Brofsky/Stockbyte/Getty Images; Right: © Jean Louis Batt/The Image Bank/Getty Images
Page 135: © Photos.com/RF
Page 137: Top: © Mark Andersen/RubberBall/Alamy; Center Top: © Photos.com/RF; Center Bottom: © IndexOpen/RF; Bottom: © Stockbyte/Getty Images

Unit 8:
Page 147: © Ian Miles – Flashpoint Pictures/Alamy
Page 150: © Photos.com/RF
Page 153: © IndexOpen/RF

Stand Out Basic Skills Index

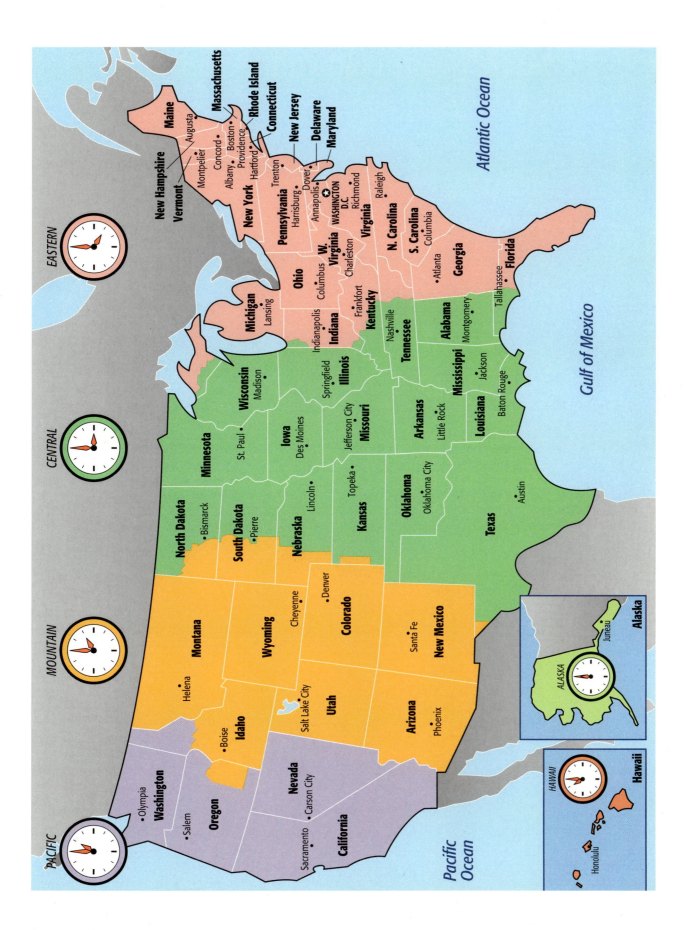

EASTERN

CENTRAL

MOUNTAIN

PACIFIC

Atlantic Ocean

Gulf of Mexico

Pacific Ocean

Maine
Augusta
New Hampshire
Vermont
Montpelier
Concord
Massachusetts
Albany • Boston
Rhode Island
Providence
Connecticut
Hartford
New Jersey
Trenton
Delaware
Maryland
Dover
Annapolis
WASHINGTON D.C.
New York
Pennsylvania
Harrisburg
Richmond
Raleigh
Virginia
N. Carolina
Columbus
Ohio
W. Virginia
Charleston
Frankfort
Kentucky
Columbia
S. Carolina
Michigan
Lansing
Indianapolis
Indiana
Nashville
Tennessee
Atlanta
Georgia
Alabama
Montgomery
Tallahassee
Florida
Wisconsin
Madison
Springfield
Illinois
Mississippi
Jackson
Minnesota
St. Paul
Iowa
Des Moines
Jefferson City
Missouri
Arkansas
Little Rock
Louisiana
Baton Rouge
North Dakota
Bismarck
South Dakota
Pierre
Nebraska
Lincoln
Topeka
Kansas
Oklahoma
Oklahoma City
Austin
Texas
Denver
Cheyenne
Colorado
Montana
Wyoming
Santa Fe
New Mexico
Helena
Salt Lake City
Utah
Arizona
Phoenix
Boise
Idaho
Nevada
Carson City
Washington
Olympia
Salem
Oregon
Sacramento
California

Alaska
Juneau
ALASKA

Hawaii
Honolulu
HAWAII